CONTEMPORARY PLAYWRIGHTS

JOHN ARDEN
BY
RONALD HAYMAN

HEINEMANN · LONDON

Heinemann Educational Books Ltd
London Edinburgh Melbourne Toronto
Singapore Johannesburg Auckland
Ibadan Hong Kong Nairobi

SBN 435 18401 6

Published by Heinemann Educational Books Ltd
48 Charles Street, London W1X 8AH
Printed in Great Britain by
Cox & Wyman Ltd, London, Fakenham and Reading

CONTENTS

ACKNOWLEDGEMENTS

The Author would like to thank Catherine Barton, Martha Crewe, John Peter, Charles Tomlinson and Irving Wardle for their help in reading typescripts and making useful comments, when the series was in preparation.

The Author and Publishers wish to thank the following for permission to include quotations from the publications listed below:

The Waters of Babylon, Live Like Pigs, The Happy Haven: John Arden and Penguin Books Ltd; *Serjeant Musgrave's Dance, Armstrong's Last Goodnight, Soldier, Soldier and Other Plays, The Business of Good Government, Ironhand, The Workhouse Donkey, Left-Handed Liberty, Friday's Hiding*: John Arden and Methuen & Co Ltd.

The photographs of *Armstrong's Last Goodnight* and *The Workhouse Donkey* are reproduced by courtesy of Angus McBean; that of *Serjeant Musgrave's Dance* by courtesy of the Royal Court Theatre.

JOHN ARDEN

Texts

Three Plays
   containing *The Waters of Babylon, Live Like Pigs* and *The Happy Haven*

This is a Penguin. *The Happy Haven* is also published in their *New English Dramatists No. 4*. Arden's other plays are published by Methuen:

Serjeant Musgrave's Dance

The Business of Good Government (written with Margaretta D'Arcy)

Ironhand

The Workhouse Donkey

Armstrong's Last Goodnight

Left-Handed Liberty

Soldier, Soldier and Other Plays
   also containing *Wet Fish, When is a Door not a Door?* and *Friday's Hiding* (with Margaretta D'Arcy)

The Royal Pardon (with Margaretta D'Arcy)

The Hero Rises Up (with Margaretta D'Arcy)

Performances

October 1957	*The Waters of Babylon* given a Sunday night production at the Royal Court directed by Graham Evans with Robert Stephens
September 1958	*Live Like Pigs* at the Royal Court directed by George Devine with Wilfred Lawson

John Arden

JOHN ARDEN

John Arden is above all a public playwright. He doesn't write out of private obsessions or personal problems. His plays are much more about relationships between groups than relationships between individuals. His characters are nearly always representatives of a group interest and they can be categorized according to their place in the community or according to the social purpose which they embody. In *Serjeant Musgrave's Dance*, there are the four soldiers who take the skeleton of a dead comrade back to his home-town in order to preach an anti-war message to the community; the mayor, the parson and the constable, who represent authority inside the town; and the colliers, Annie and the landlady who stand for the ordinary townspeople, the victims of authority. In *Live Like Pigs* there are the gypsies, the respectable neighbours and the representatives of civil government. In *The Workhouse Donkey*, Arden himself divides his cast list up under four headings: Labour, Conservative, the Police, and the Electorate. And you could go through all his plays, grouping the characters up in this way.

Some of them still emerge very strongly as individuals, even if their personality is secondary to what they stand for. Talking about Serjeant Musgrave to the editors of *Encore*, Arden said:

> I decided what he had to say, and why he had to say it, and roughly what he was going to do about it, before I worked out the character. The character came to fit the actions. I am always being told this is the wrong way to write a play. But with *Serjeant Musgrave* I thought: assume that an army sergeant in a colonial war is sufficiently disgusted with a particular atrocity he has been involved in. He comes back to England to make a demonstration of protest. I don't know at that stage the details of the demonstration, they're not worked out in my mind – well, what sort of man is he likely to be? Granted the period – I began with the scarlet uniforms for purely theatrical reasons – I used my historical imagination, and decided that the most likely character would be one of those Crimean Sergeants, who fought with rifle in one hand, and bible in the other. This is not a character I

1

John Arden

feel particularly sympathetic to – but he seemed to be a plausible historical type.

Only one of the colliers in the play, Walsh, is given a name. The others, as in a Ben Jonson comedy of manners, are described as 'a bashful collier' and 'a slow collier'. The same thing very nearly happened with the soldiers.

> I started off calling them 'One Soldier', 'Two Soldier', and 'Three Soldier', wrote a few scenes, decided they were developing certain characteristics of their own, went back and renamed them 'The Joking Soldier', 'The Surly Soldier', and 'The Grey-Haired Soldier'. I finished the play and then when we went into rehearsal decided they had better have names – this was really Lindsay Anderson's idea. He maintained that if you call a character 'The Surly Soldier', it is going to make an actor think he has got to be surly all the way through. It was not until they had names that the soldiers really came alive as people.

Arden is alone among dramatists of today in trying to see a community as a whole. This is what Shakespeare did of course, not only in the histories but in the tragedies too. The king is the actual head of the community. His health, mental and physical, isn't just symbolic of the well-being of the country, but materially relevant to it. If a bad king succeeds a good king, in Hamlet's Denmark for example, a moral deterioration ensues, which seems to affect the whole country. Of course a modern political state is much too complex a unit to be written about in this way, which is why Arden sets so much of his action on the level of local, rather than national, politics.

In his first play (or the first to be produced) *The Waters of Babylon*, he sets the action in North London and tries to work out many issues of national importance in local terms. We have the local M.P., a local councillor, Hyde Park orators and so on, but Arden was taking on too much, even for one of the thickly textured plots that he delights in, and his later plays are all set in a town away from the centre, so that it can more easily become – or seem to become – a separate unit. In *Serjeant Musgrave's Dance*, the town is cut off from the rest of England because the canal freezes over, so until the grenadiers arrive like a *deus ex machina* it is literally a self-contained community. And in *The Workhouse Donkey*, Arden treats the town

2

in very much the same way. Of course, it isn't just in order to create a self-sufficient society. It's also to have a manœuvrable microcosm of the country as a whole, though it isn't always a satisfactory microcosm even for Arden's purposes. For him, the corruption on the town council is representative of corruption on the top level of our whole society, which is why such a high proportion of his characters are either town councillors or civil servants. But the villainy of characters like Butterthwaite doesn't always seem sufficiently relevant to the inadequacies of politicians in power on a higher level.

Not being primarily interested in personality, Arden doesn't write star parts. Serjeant Musgrave and Gilnockie (in *Armstrong's Last Goodnight*), which are two of the best parts he's written, are both quite small in terms of the number of lines that the leading character has. Not surprisingly, the meatiest part of all is a king – John in *Left-Handed Liberty*. But if there's seldom a dominating figure in the foreground, he goes a long way towards making up for it with the lively detail in the background. His Brueghel-like canvasses teem with physical life and a very warm sympathy penetrates into the oddest corners of the social scene. Arden identifies equally well with the rich elderly inmates of *The Happy Haven* and the ageing gypsies making love in *Live Like Pigs*.

> RACHEL: And red eyes: and a bad leg, too . . . Hey then, hold it out. I'll rub it till it's better. Oh me poor old horse. (*She massages his leg, singing*)
> Poor old horse, poor old horse.
> SAILOR (*sings*): Poor old horse, poor old horse.
> COL (*waking up in the small bedroom and shouting*): Shut the bloody row!

Alongside his extraordinary sociological sensitivity goes an extraordinary historical sense. Neither Robert Bolt nor John Osborne – nor any of the other recent writers who have attempted historical subjects – have a historical imagination like Arden's. He thinks naturally in historical terms, even in his contemporary plays. But he isn't primarily interested in accuracy. In the preface to *Serjeant Musgrave's Dance*, he describes how the soldiers in the Royal Court production 'wore the scarlet tunics and spiked helmets

John Arden

characteristic of the later (or 'Kipling') epoch, while the Constable was dressed in tall hat and tail coat as an early Peeler – his role in the play suggesting a rather primitive type of police organization'. But what he always achieves unfailingly in the writing is the right flavour. Whatever the anomalies and the anachronisms, we believe in the feel of the period that he evokes.

As with Brecht, part of his reason for going to history is to achieve a distance from the contemporary scene that enables him to comment on it all the more pointedly. *Armstrong's Last Goodnight* was partly inspired by Connor Cruise O'Brien's book on the Congo, *To Katanga and Back,* and one of the things that sparked off *Serjeant Musgrave's Dance* was an incident in Cyprus.

> A soldier's wife was shot in the street by terrorists – and according to newspaper reports – which was all I had to work on at the time – some soldiers ran wild at night and people were killed in the rounding-up. The atrocity which sparks off Musgrave's revolt, and which happens before the play begins, is roughly similar.

To what extent is Arden writing in order to change his audience? In fact his approach is quite well characterized by Brecht's description of the difference between his 'Epic Theatre' and the conventional 'Dramatic Theatre'.

> The spectator of the *dramatic* theatre says: 'Yes, I have felt the same. I am just like this. This is only natural. It will always be like this. This human being's suffering moves me because there is no way out for him. This is great art; it bears the mark of the inevitable. I am weeping with those who weep on the stage, laughing with those who laugh.'
> The spectator of the *epic* theatre says: 'I should never have thought so. That is not the way to do it. This is most surprising, hardly credible. This will have to stop. This human being's suffering moves me because there would have been a way out for him. This is great art; nothing here seems inevitable. I am laughing about those who weep on the stage, weeping about those who laugh.'

Serjeant Musgrave's Dance is, like Mother Courage, a simultaneous demonstration of the idiocy of war and of people's inability to learn how idiotic it is.

> I'll tell you for what a soldier's good:
> To march behind his roaring drum,
> Shout to us all: 'Here I come
> I've killed as many as I could –
> I'm stamping into your fat town
> From the war and to the war
> And every girl can be my whore
> Just watch me lay them squealing down.'
> And that's what he does and so do we.
> Because we know he'll soon be dead
> We strap our arms round the scarlet red
> Then send him weeping over the sea.
> Oh he will go and a long long way.
> Before he goes we'll make him pay
> Between the night and the next cold day –
> By God there's a whole lot more I could say –
> What good's a bloody soldier 'cept to be dropped into a slit in
> the ground like a letter in a box. How many did you bring with
> you – is it four?

Funnily enough the most Brechtian characteristic in Arden's work is his dependence on the tradition of English ballad opera. Both playwrights have their characters sliding in and out of songs and rhymes in a way that makes us look at them as if through the wrong end of a telescope. In Brecht this is a deliberate alienation effect; in Arden it is a deep-seated habit, corresponding to the way he thinks. And sometimes, as in Annie's rhyme, it helps, unrealistically, to give an effect of period authenticity, as if the language had a lifeline going back to the popular speech of a hundred years ago.

Arden's use of verse in the theatre is quite different from T. S. Eliot's. Far from wanting the audience to be unaware that it's verse that they're hearing, he wants the transitions from prose to verse to be clearly marked.

> The ancient Irish heroic legends were told at dinner as prose tales, of invariable content but, in the manner of their telling, improvised to suit the particular occasion or the poet's mood.

John Arden

When, however, he arrived at one of the emotional climaxes of the story such as the lament of Deirdre for the Sons of Usna or the sleep-song of Grainne over Diarmaid, then he would sing a poem which he had by heart and which was always the same. So in a play, the dialogue can be naturalistic and 'plotty' as long as the basic poetic issue has not been crystallized. But when this point is reached, then the language becomes formal (if you like, in verse, or sung), the visual pattern coalesces into a visual image that is one of the nerve-centres of the play.

Sometimes this works very well, as it does with Annie's rhyme. But sometimes he derives situations in his plays too directly from the simple basic themes of the ballad tradition. The girl in *Armstrong's Last Goodnight,* for instance, who leaves her family and takes to the forest because they've killed her lover, is a character who belongs to a ballad. She very nearly *is* a ballad.

> Are ye comen, my wearie dearie,
> Are ye comen, my lovely hinnie,
> I will find ye a wee bracken bush
> To keep the north wind frae aff your ancient body.

Lyrically this is pleasing and effective but ballad situations are stock situations and stock situations encourage scamped motivations. Sometimes they don't matter, but often, as with this girl, they do.

THE WATERS OF BABYLON

The Waters of Babylon was given a Sunday-night production at the Royal Court in October 1957 with Robert Stephens as Krank. It was a very bad production, which is a pity, because it's a play that might otherwise have made quite a strong impact, though it could never have succeeded completely, however well it had been stylized.

It's a racy, picaresque plot, with a thick, coarse texture of incidents. At first sight, it looks as though it might have been more suited to film treatment, with its rich assortment of characters, its quick changes of locale, and its far-fetched, thriller-like adventures. Sigismanfred Krankiewicz, the hero, is leading a triple life. He's a pimp, a Rachman-type landlord, and every morning, after changing his clothes in the gentlemen's lavatory in Baker Street station, where the attendant is one of his tenants, he goes to work in an architect's office. In spite of the three sources of income, he's broke and very hard put to it to raise the five hundred pounds he owes to Paul, another Pole, who threatens to assemble a bomb in his house unless the money is repaid to him by the end of next month. Paul wants to blow up Bulganin and Kruschev on their visit to London; Krank, who's been in Buchenwald, wants to have nothing further to do with politics. Krank has made contact with a shifty north country ex-mayor, Butterthwaite, thinking that his experience of local government and of the 'tricks and traps of English bureaucracy' will be helpful in warding off the interest that the local council is taking in his lodging house. Eighty people are living there and the tenants have to pay five shillings extra each time someone spends the night with them.

Butterthwaite concocts a scheme for a municipal lottery which is to be presented to the local council as Krank's idea, and when the need for £500 becomes urgent, they decide to rig the draw. The moving spirit behind the local council's acceptance of the scheme is Joe Caligula, a coloured Councillor who's been sleeping with Bathsheba – a West Indian tart who works for Krank and lives in his house. She is chosen – with no more implausibility than any-

John Arden

thing else – to pick the ticket out of the drum at the draw and Krank and Butterthwaite have arranged with Cassidy, the Irish lavatory attendant, that when he hears the clash of cymbals that signals the moment of the draw, he's to pull a switch in the basement that will plunge the building into darkness. In the blackout, Butterthwaite will put a counterfoil into Bathsheba's hand of a ticket which has been bought by Cassidy's sister, an ex-girl-friend of Krank's and now the mistress of the local M.P., from whom she hopes to graduate to a Cabinet minister.

There are still more strands in the plot, which are joined together through similar coincidences. The M.P. is building a house for Teresa Cassidy and wants to have it designed by the architect who is employing Krank. She has also had an affair with him and now the M.P. falls in love with her. Together they turn up at the draw, where Butterthwaite is too drunk to play his part properly and everything goes wrong. He crawls out from under a table in his mayor's costume and the lottery is won by the wife of the policeman who's been sent along to ensure fair play. The M.P. orders him to arrest Krank, but he can't because when the telephone rings, instead of the news the M.P. was expecting that the bomb had been found in Krank's house, the news we hear is that the bomb has mysteriously vanished. Henry Ginger, a Hyde Park orator who is running a semi-Empire-Loyalist campaign against foreigners, finds that Krank was in Buchenwald not as a prisoner but as a guard and he's also found out about the bomb. Paul finally appears at the meeting and, aiming to shoot Henry Ginger, accidentally hits Krank, who has a dying speech in rhymed couplets which ties up most of the threads that are still loose in the plot.

> The bomb, Cassidy, I think you stole it.
> I hope your brave boys can control it,
> For is it not the nature of such ammunition
> To perpetuate partition?
> Of your sister imagine no more evil.
> She is now reaching Ministerial level.
> So use respect. Good-bye, Charlie.
> A pity the cymbals have had to clang so early.
> Your Hundred Days were short I fear.

The Waters of Babylon

Ladies, come here . . .
. Bathsheba, Teresa, Barbara – Miss Baulkfast:
I'm going to declare my identity at last.
Place and time, and purposes,
Are now to be chosen for me.
I cannot any longer do without knowing them . . .

Altogether the play has contained an incredibly complex mass of
themes and Arden showed a considerable architectural talent in
building them together as well as he did.

But though his approach to plot in this early play must derive to
some extent from his film-going, *The Waters of Babylon* couldn't have
made a film. Not that its demands on the audience's credulity are any
more excessive than in say, a James Bond film, but the plot is much
too confusing and, in any case, Arden's interest isn't really in the
story as such. The private lives of the characters are threaded through
the public events, which interest him much more, and the play as a
whole is more of a personal statement than is provided by thriller
films, even the best of which, like Hitchcock's, have a smooth
anonymity of manner. The trouble is that *The Waters of Babylon*
doesn't finally achieve any unity of style or convention. It
dabbles for too long in too many different ones, often letting different
characters speak as if they were parts of different plays. We have the
stage Irish of the Cassidy brother and sister, the florid West Indian
images of Caligula and Bathsheba, and the jumbled cadences of
Polish-English.

> Half past seven of a morning. What kind of day is it? Cold, I
> think, yes, cold, rainy, foggy, perhaps by dinner-time it will
> snow. No? Perhaps not snow, it is after all spring. March, April,
> May, even in London. I do not think – even in North London,
> perhaps, not snow. Breakfast, what sort of breakfast, this coffee
> it is not very fresh, is it? After the nature of an archaeological
> deposit, more water more coffee into the pot every morning, but
> at the bottom it has been there six weeks, seven, it's like drinking
> bitumen. Why don't I wash my cups and plates more often than
> only once a week?' Cause I am a man of filthy habits in my
> house, is why.

We have songs, blank verse and the rhymed verse of Krank's dying speech, which is rather like the epilogue of an eighteenth-century play. It even takes on suddenly a moral tone, which is a clear case of the manner conditioning the matter, for it's quite out of character for Krank, dying or not, and ironic or not.

> Let the Bolshevik tyrants arrive:
> Conviviality shall thrive
> And the ceaseless peace no doubt ensue.
> Councillor, that quick girl with you tried with me to cheat you, true.
> Forgive her. She had a clever master:
> But I'm almost sure you now can trust her.

On the other hand, it's not at all out of character for Arden or the play.

Altogether the play is interesting not so much for giving early examples of techniques that Arden was to refine later and not so much for statements of themes or its introduction of characters that he was later to refer to, but for its experiments with language. Sometimes the language is clogged and clumsy, sometimes it's oversimplified, as in these rhymed couplets. Sometimes it lapses into very odd blank verse and sometimes it rises to a lyric simplicity, which is very touching, as in Krank's dying words.

> So many thousands of people
> In a so large a cold field.
> How did they get into it?
> And what do they expect to find?

But even when it's bad, the dialogue never goes dead. There's an obstinate liveliness in it. However much the mind rebels with incredulity against the plot, the ears responds to the texture – thick or thin – in the writing.

SOLDIER, SOLDIER

Soldier, Soldier, Arden's next play, was written for television. It's a strange script with most of the characters speaking mainly in prose but the central character speaking mostly in a rough, very unpoetic blank verse.

> Were *we* ever in Germany!
> Who were the boys
> Set Düsseldorf Naafi club on fire?
> Who stole the Burgomaster's daughter
> Out of Bacharach-on-Rhine?
> There was a song made over that:
> I'm going to sing it to yous.
> Shut your mouths, every man.

The difference between his language and theirs reflects the difference between the type of person he is and the type they are. Unlike most Arden characters, who are representative of the background we see them against, the Soldier is violently different from the townsmen, and this is the point of the play. He's strident and disorderly, while they are quiet and conformist. He's a likeable rogue, while they are benightedly honest. He enjoys life in a way that would always get him into trouble, while they keep out of trouble at the cost of having nothing to enjoy. The town is a bleak northern industrial town, very much like the town in *Serjeant Musgrave's Dance,* but contemporary. There's not so much as usual this time about local politics, though one of the characters, Joe Parker, hopes to get on to the Borough Council and wants to make use of information he's picked up from the Soldier in his campaign to get himself elected. But this is a side-issue. The main plot revolves round the Scuffhams, a pious, puritanical window-cleaner and his wife, whose son is in the same regiment as the Soldier. They haven't heard from him for two years so they're quite prepared to swallow the cock-and-bull story that the Soldier tells them about him. He says that the boy's in the glasshouse, but that if they give him enough money he will be able to pay witnesses for a new trial. Actually he doesn't know Tommy

John Arden

Scuffham at all, but they're gullible enough to give up their bedroom to him and give him their savings. He also makes love to Tommy's wife, who's been living all this time with her parents-in-law, waiting for Tommy to come back.

From the opening moment, when the Soldier bursts into the shabby little railway pub, Arden obviously enjoys his anarchical behaviour, very much in the same way that he was later to enjoy the Sawneys' and Gilnockie's.

> SOLDIER (*suddenly lifts his chin and bellows*): Git on Parade!
> (*All the talking stops.*)
> One-two-three, two-two-three, Three!
> (*He beats both fists on the bar, and shouts all in a gabble.*)
> Who comes here?
> A Fusilier,
> What does he want?
> He wants his beer.
> Where's his money?
> Here's his money.
> (*He tosses a pocketful of miscellaneous money on to the bar, and exhorts the Landlord.*)
> Smarten it up, mucker, there's a soldier wants his drink.

Of course this isn't to say that Arden necessarily approves either of the Soldier's truculence here or of his unscrupulousness later, but certainly he sees him as embodying the vitality and virility which the townspeople lack. We're made to feel that it's not just the Scuffhams but the whole town that will be the poorer when he's gone.

While emphasizing the difference between the Soldier and everyone else in the town, the writing shows very little interest on Arden's part in differentiating between the other characters. Mary, the wife, emerges quite sharply, though mentally she appears far more alert in some incidents than in others, but the Scuffhams and the Parkers are fairly flat and uncharacterized. Parker in particular is an unsatisfactory creation. He has quite a big role to play, taking the Soldier along to the Scuffhams and encouraging them to give him money, but he always seems to be doing what the plot requires him to do, not what he actually would do. In some ways he's a bit like the Bargee in *Serjeant Musgrave's Dance*, who also has to help the plot along, but the Bargee's actions are motivated quite convincingly by self-interest and his dialogue has a pungent irony in it which is quite lacking in Parker's.

The play often reminds us of *Serjeant Musgrave's Dance,* and in fact it wasn't televised until after *Serjeant Musgrave's Dance* had been produced. Scuffham is made the spokesman for many of the samen preoccupations that we find in the later play.

> Them as takes up sword has to perish by sword. When he went for a regular soldier, he threw up everything I tried to learn him. It's what your husband says, Mrs Parker, Force and Colonialism: that's how he stands now: and strike-breaking and all that.

And

> You can go back to your murdering and your trampling on Sovereign Rights of independent folk, and your shooting-down of working men in the streets: but as far as this house goes, you're done and you're capped.

But these elements aren't very well integrated into the plot.

The best scene in the play is the final scene between the Soldier (who's never given a name) and Mary, who's decided she wants to marry him.

> MARY: I have no more life left for Tommy; all of my life is for you.
>
> SOLDIER: Is that so –
>
> MARY: I'm telling you no lies, boy.
>
> SOLDIER (*furiously*): Nor I'm telling you none neither! God help us, a soldier's wife. D'ye imagine I've never met ye before, hell's devil eat your feet, woman – I *married* ye in Birmingham nineteen forty-one! I've tickled your pretty wee lugs and chuckled into your armpits in London and Fort George and Glasgow and Düsseldorf and Naples and Sidi Barrani, and ye're worse each time than the last and it's this bloody time ye're the worst of bloody all.

This is a kind of insight that belongs very much to the ballad tradition. Arden sees all the lowest common multiples in human experience. At moments like this, the man is every soldier there has ever been and the girl is every soldier's wife.

LIVE LIKE PIGS

Live Like Pigs is a less ambitious play than *Serjeant Musgrave's Dance*, but it fulfils its ambition more completely than that or any other Arden play. It's the most naturalistic play he's written and except for the ballad-like verses that introduce most of the seventeen scenes, and except for the occasional song, it's written almost entirely in prose. But suddenly, Arden has found absolute clarity of focus and consistency of style. For the first time, he's a master of his material. In *The Waters of Babylon* and *Soldier, Soldier,* the unevennesses in the writing and the difficulties for the audience both derive from the same failure to see the whole field of the action in the same perspective. In *Live Like Pigs,* there are no stereotypes in the characterization, no jolts in the rhythm of the action and no bad patches in the writing. The dialogue is pitched perfectly throughout, controlled, economical and richly flavoured.

This time there's no central figure in the action. There's a central group – Sailor Sawney, Big Rachel, his woman, Rosie, his daughter, and Col, Rachel's son. With Rosie's two children, Sally and the baby, they're herded out of a broken tram-car on a caravan site, where they've been living, into a council house. They are contrasted with their neighbours in rather the same way as the Soldier is with the townsmen: in an area of unimaginative respectability, they embody all the Dionysiac virtues. They break all the rules, they steal, they insult the neighbours, they enjoy promiscuous sex, they don't keep their house clean, they get drunk, and they refuse to send Sally to school. Arden sees them as descendants of the 'sturdy beggars' of the sixteenth century, with values that derive from a nomadic existence. They have been crowded out of the open spaces, where they belong, by the proliferating buildings that have encroached farther and farther into the country, suppressing the freedom of the old life as they spread the suspect civilization of the new. The Sawneys end up, as they're bound to, by being turned out of the housing estate by the local authorities, whose actions reflect the feelings of the outraged neighbours. But our sympathy is with the Sawneys and, as at

the end of *Soldier, Soldier,* Arden makes us feel that the neighbour-
hood will be quieter, more peaceful, but distinctly worse off without
them.

His achievement in inventing a language for the Sawneys is a very
considerable one. He forges a vernacular for them which sounds
illiterate but expresses everything he needs it to. It also sounds
outlandish but, unlike the language in *Armstrong's Last Goodnight,* it's
not difficult for the audience to understand. It's salty, often bordering
on the poetic, and the crowded rhythms are like young animals in a
confined space leaping for food, but they pack in the meaning breath-
lessly and colloquially.

> ROSIE (*white with anger*): You bring that Daffodil here?
> BLACKMOUTH (*reasonable and pleading*): Well now, what else?
> Look: they wor after her in Macclesfield, see. So I meet up
> with them, chancy, on the road, the Old Croaker's half-daft:
> where are they going, what are they to do? See, Daffodil:
> like, poorly – I don't know what, she's *poorly*. And then there's
> some of them Scotchmen we met, you know, Jocky Faa with
> the one eye, his lot – through here Tuesday with their wagon,
> he says they've been giving to you Sawneys a right living house
> here, warm and roof and all . . . You're not going to turn us out
> now. Why, Daffodil's gone all wrong. And with travelling
> nights and all. We come here on a lorry. Spewing sick every
> mile.
> SAILOR (*still hard*): Bring her in.
> BLACKMOUTH (*relieved*): Ah well, you've room enough I knew
> it.
> SAILOR: Blackmouth clever-mouth, aren't ye?

This is ballad-like in its combination of approximation and precision.

After *The Waters of Babylon* and *Soldier, Soldier,* it's a big and
pleasant surprise that Arden manages to bring so many different
characters so vividly to life, differentiating so well between them and
giving each of them such a good share of the foreground. The most
dominating character is Sailor, but he's seventy, too old to dominate
unchallenged. Rachel, who's forty, sometimes manages to overrule
him and Col, who's just growing into manhood, sometimes gets his
own way. Blackmouth is twenty-eight but he's an outsider to the

15

John Arden

central party. As Arden says in his preface, 'The Old Croaker-Blackmouth-Daffodil group have much the same effect upon Sailor's household as the Sawneys in general do upon the Jacksons' (the respectable neighbours). Blackmouth is half gypsy and the father of Rosie's children. Daffodil is his seventeen-year-old girl-friend who later becomes Col's girl-friend. The Old Croaker is her mother. As uninvited guests they get the Sawneys into more trouble with the neighbours and the police than they're in already. The Old Croaker enjoys tearing up washing from clothes-lines. Blackmouth knifes a local policeman. Daffodil brings a doctor into the house, who is appalled at its condition. But the doctor, the police sergeant and the official from the housing department are characterized sympathetically and shown to be sympathetic, while the next door neighbours are very much more than incarnations of local lower-middle-class conformity.

From the beginning, Arden succeeds in picking on the right small incidents to symbolize the frictions that start off by being trivial but grow much too big for the Sawneys to survive. The first petty quarrel is between Rosie and the council official. She tells him that he has no right to chase Sally out of the house just because the child was running water in the bathroom. The official points out that she'd left the plug in the basin and water was going all over the floor. When Sailor arrives he immediately celebrates the fact of having a house by ordering the official out of it.

> Here we are and here we've got to live. But we're keeping *them* out from us, every bloody one of them. (*He stands astride and terrible.*) They call me Sailor Sawney and no man slaps his natter at *me*.

In defending Sailor against Rachel, who says he ought to get a job, Rosie shows us her (and Arden's) admiration for the old man's anarchical virility.

> There's no one can touch that old Sailor once he's got his strength in. My mam, when she wor living, he'd be out on a job, wind a crane, dig drains, heaving barrels, what you like, all day he'd be at it; then into the boozer til closing – likely fight a pair o' men into canal dock, knock a copper over after – then home like a

traction engine and revel her three times down to Rio without
he'd even take off his boots.

Often the situations that crop up in the action are very common-
place – the inquisitve neighbour putting on a show of trying to be
friendly, Col trying to persuade her daughter, Doreen, to come to
the Palais with him – but the pace is rapid, the texture is thick and
the incidents are varied. The play never strikes us as a social play in
which episodes are chosen to illustrate contemporary social history.
They do in fact do just that, but there's enough life in them to take
their illustrative functions in their stride. And again, as in *The Waters
of Babylon,* we see Arden's talent for weaving a large number of
thematic strands very tightly together. Sally idolizes both Col and
Blackmouth. Col uses her as a messenger to take tools that he steals
from the building site, where he works, to a fence. Coming home
from one of these journeys, she tells Col how she used Blackmouth
as a threat in order to get the man's price up.

> SALLY: He warn't going to let me have more nor a quid, Col;
> but I says to him, I says: 'Col says my dad Blackmouth's home
> and he did a Screw right dead and if you don't give me more
> nor two quid he'll do you too, good and proper,' I tell him. So
> he give me thirty bob for 'em. Here, see. (*She gives him the
> money.*)
> COL (*vexed*): T't t't – not much, wor it? O.K. kid, you buy you
> some spice. O.K. (*He gives her a couple of coins back.*)
> SALLY (*in delight*): Eee Col! . . . Is my dad back?

More than in any of the other plays, Arden's warmth extends to
all his characters. In one scene there's a knife-fight between Blackmouth and Col over Daffodil. Blackmouth runs away, leaving Col,
the boy, feeling like a man. He puts his favourite record on the
gramophone to celebrate – 'Cigarettes and Whiskey and Wild, Wild
Women'. Sailor comes in and orders him to turn the music off.
Sailor then proves that Daffodil isn't really ill by biting her on the
fore-arm, she reacts by aiming a furious swipe at his head – a sure
sign of health. He then tries to throw her and her mother out of the
house and confronts Col with a beer bottle when the boy challenges
his authority. Then Big Rachel intervenes.

John Arden

RACHEL: Let him be, Sailor. He wants his tart – he can have his tart, why shouldn't he? He's my lad, he's a mind and rights of his own.

SAILOR (*after a pause, lowering the bottle*): Ah, so. The young man cries for his rights and the old man carries the load. Well, live and let live. I'm asking nowt more nor that for *me* – so I'm as well to serve it to *you*, I dare say. Go on, Daffy, you bide. Till he breaks your neck. Heh heh.

All through the seventeen scenes, with their profuse variety of incidents, the dramatic tension is kept taut, with quick changes of subject and mood. We get a rich feeling of life being lived out to the full in front of us. The warm smell of the Sawneys fills the theatre. But the best scenes of all, with the most imaginative use of the stage, come at the end of the play, when the house is being besieged by the neighbours, whose accumulation of anger has boiled over. Col is practically torn to peices by the indignant women of the housing estate, who think he tried to rape Doreen. Bricks are thrown through the window and we hear the furious voices of the crowd outside. Rachel disperses them by yelling at them threateningly but when Sailor goes out to reconnoitre he comes back bleeding from the side of his head, where he's been hit by a stone. They barricade themselves in as best they can but a big mob gathers outside and the feeling of siege is made very real. After a sleepless night, the Sawneys are saved only by the arrival of the police. But the sergeant finds a drill that Col has stolen and he has to jump out through a window to escape. In trying to delay the policeman who's pursuing him, Sailor breaks his bad leg in the scuffle. Rachel picks up her bundle and walks out, leaving him moaning on the floor, waiting for an ambulance to come, while the policeman and the housing official stand over him. This is the ending that Arden's plays so often have – the forces of chaos routed and order restored. It's also the ending that Shakespeare's histories and tragedies often have, with the battle over and the villain destroyed. But in Arden, we never have more than a very limited sympathy with the victors. Shakespeare was satisfied with the *status quo*; since Arden is not, he does not necessarily see the restoration of order as a good thing.

SERJEANT MUSGRAVE'S DANCE

Like *Live Like Pigs, Serjeant Musgrave's Dance* still hasn't been seen in the West End, but it's been put on twice at the Royal Court. In October 1959, Lindsay Anderson directed it with designs by Jocelyn Herbert and with Ian Bannen, Frank Finlay, Alan Dobie, Donal Donelly, Freda Jackson, Patsy Byrne, Stratford Johns, Colin Blakely and James Bree in the cast. The controversy that the production started built up too slowly to save it and it died after twenty-eight performances, to be revived six years later in a production which didn't make anything like as much impact. As Musgrave, Iain Cuthbertson lacked Ian Bannen's taut, tortured compulsiveness and most of the other parts were played by actors who couldn't compete with their predecessors, whose performances had left such a clear mark in the memory.

Serjeant Musgrave's Dance is conceived on a bigger scale than *Live Like Pigs* and ultimately it displays more of Arden's individuality, but it's more eclectic in its origins. It owes a great deal to Brecht's version of *The Recruiting Officer – Drums and Trumpets* – and Arden has described how he got some hints for setting up the structure of the play from an American film called *The Raid*. 'The plan of the film is rather similar: a group of men – Confederate soldiers in disguise – ride into a Northern town . . . On the appointed morning they all turn out in their Confederate uniforms, hoist a flag in the square, rob the bank and burn the houses. Finally, as in *Serjeant Musgrave,* the cavalry arrives at the last minute although in this case they are too late.' Ronald Bryden suggested in the *New Statesman* that the play also had unconscious roots in the miracle plays, Housman, Auden, John Whiting's *Saint's Day* and Tennyson's *Vision of Sin.* Nevertheless, it's a much more unconventional play than *Live Like Pigs* and it gave Arden's dramatic imagination much more freedom to articulate itself in the stage imagery.

The excitement of *Live Like Pigs* depends on individual and group inter-relationships: the stage picture only contributes to the tension at the end, when the house is in a state of siege. In *Serjeant Musgrave's*

Dance the visual and the verbal excitements are inseparable. The action moves freely from place to place, often in the open air, and each scene has a starkly etched opening.

The play starts with the soldiers at the beginning of their journey into the coal-mining country. They're squatting round a drum, playing cards and speaking lines that are full of references to the symbolic colours that are in front of us on the stage and ahead of us in the action – red uniforms against the white sky, red and black cards, Black Jack Musgrave, the red of blood and the black of coal-dust and death. In the second scene, the lights go up on a public bar in which the only drinker is a parson; the third scene opens with Hurst whistling nervously in a churchyard. Nor does Arden waste the atmosphere that he achieves with these opening moments. The blackness of the visual effects fuses with the blackness of what's going on, with the soldiers on their mad and murderous mission in the mining town, where the communications are all cut – the roads blocked, the canal frozen and the telegraph put out of action by the snow. The plot pulses grimly towards its moments of climax, which also make a strong visual impact – Musgrave praying in the churchyard, his hands crossed on his chest, with the grotesque figure of the Bargee behind him, parodying his movements and his words and, above all, the moment in the market-place when Attercliffe hoists up the skeleton of the dead soldier in his tattered red uniform. Musgrave immediately does his 'dance'.

> Up he goes and no one knows
> How to bring him downwards
> Dead man's feet
> Over the street
> Riding the roofs
> And crying down your chimneys.

Serjeant Musgrave's Dance was Arden's first departure from the present into the past and his imagination was more liberated than confined by it. With most of the other recent playwrights who have attempted historical subjects, Whiting, Osborne and Robert Bolt for example, we find that it encourages any tendencies they have to write in a heroic vein. In *The Devils, Luther* and *A Man for All*

Seasons, we get a line-up of the heroic protagonist against everyone else, one man isolated against the time he's living in, and the more this happens, the more the hero tends to emerge as a modern figure. Arden is different from these writers not only because he has a better historical imagination, but also because he's less concerned with a central individual. In *Serjeant Musgrave's Dance,* as in *Live Like Pigs,* what we get is a central group and, again as in *Live Like Pigs,* it's not at all held up for our admiration. The soldiers are all deserters, Hurst has killed an officer, Attercliffe is a mournful cuckold and Musgrave has stolen from the regiment.

Unfortunately, though, these points are planted rather late and rather clumsily. In *Live Like Pigs,* Arden found no difficulty at all in telling us what we needed to know about the characters in the order we needed to know it. The story unrolled quickly and effortlessly with the right degree of inevitability and the right spacing between actions and their consequences. In *Serjeant Musgrave's Dance,* the development is much slower and Arden seems to be up against a difficulty that troubled him in *The Waters of Babylon* and *Soldier, Soldier* – the problem of how and when to plant the plot points that need to be planted. In the first scene, he's uncertain about how obvious it ought to be to the audience that the soldiers have a skeleton in one of their boxes. There's nothing explicit, only dark hints which are bound to be worrying unless you know the play already.

> SPARKY: Ha, there's nobody to hear us. You're safe as a bloody blockhouse out here – I'm on the sentry, boy, *I'm* your protection.
>
> ATTERCLIFFE (*irritably*): You make sure you are then. Go on: keep watching.
>
> SPARKY (*returns to his guard*): Ah. Ha-ha . . . Or did you think *he* could hear you? (*He gestures towards the boxes.*) Maybe, maybe . . . *I* thought I heard him laugh.
>
> ATTERCLIFFE: Steady, boy.
>
> SPARKY (*a little wildly*): Steady yourself, you crumbling old cuckold. He might laugh, who knows? Well, make a rattling any road. Mightn't he, soldier boy?

He also confuses us deliberately and misguidedly about the object

John Arden

of the soldiers' visit to the town. Whether they're really recruiting or not remains a mystery until the third scene and then their objectives are made rather too explicit, with the soldiers telling each other what they already know.

MUSGRAVE: One night's work in the streets of one city, and it damned all four of us and the war it was part of. We're each one guilty of particular blood. We've come to this town to work that guilt back to where it began.

(*He turns to Sparky.*)

Why to this town? Say it, say it!

SPARKY (*as with a conditioned reflex*): Billy. Billy's dead. He wor my mucker, back end of the rear rank. He wor killed dead. He came from this town.

MUSGRAVE (*relentless*): Go on.

SPARKY (*appealing*): Serjeant –

MUSGRAVE: Use your clear brain, man, and tell me what you're doing here! Go on.

SPARKY (*incoherent with recollecting what he wants to forget*): I'm doing here? I'm doing . . . Serjeant, you know it. 'Cos he died. That wor Billy. I got drunk. Four days and four nights. After work of one night. Absent. Not sober. Improperly dressed.

(*He tries to turn it into one of his jokes.*)

Stick me in a cell, boys,
Pull the prison bell
Black Jack Musgrave
To call the prison roll –

Sarnt, no offence – 'First ye'll serve your punishment' he says. 'Then I'll show you how,' he says, the Serjeant. I says, 'You'll show me what?' He says, 'I'll show you how your Billy can be paid for' . . . I didn't want to pay for him – what had I to care for a colonial war? . . .

(*He meets Musgrave's eye and takes a grip on his motives.*)

But I *did* want to pay for him, didn't I? 'Cos that's why I'm here. 'You go down, I'll follow' . . . You, Serjeant, ent it?

Black Jack Musgrave
He always calls the roll.

He says:

Go down to Billy's town
Tell 'em how he died.

22

> And that's what I'm doing here. The Serjeant pays the fare.
> Here I am, I'm paid for. Next turn's for Billy. Or all that's
> left of Billy. Who'll give me an offer for his bones? Sixpence for
> a bone, for a bone of my dead mucker . . .

This passage pulls Sparky's characterization badly out of shape. Of
all the characters, he was the one who sprang most readily to life –
friendly, bright, nervous, the most volatile of the soldiers, always
joking and telling stories, afraid of silence and afraid of thinking, the
sort of bore who's 'the life and soul of the party'. But in this passage
the stage directions reveal an insecurity in the writing. Arden uses
the 'conditioned reflex', the jokey rhymes and the way Musgrave is
intimidating Sparky to cover up the fact that Sparky isn't just going
out of character in this passage but that he's out of character in
being involved with the others at all.

But then immediately we have to stop to ask whether he or any
of the other characters are 'characters' at all in this sense. Arden
we know, isn't primarily interested in the psychology of motivations.
The characterization is tailored to fit the actions and the actions are
the incarnations of an idea, a feeling, a protest. With Musgrave
himself, the feeling of guilt is a very plausible one and his belief that
all four of them are damned because of 'one night's work in the streets
of one town' is very good dramatic material, if only Arden were
interested in exploiting it. But he doesn't let Musgrave's actions be
determined by this feeling of damnation or by the inspiration
Musgrave thinks he's getting from God. His actions are always
determined by the requirements of the plot and there's no room left
for any freedom of decision for him or even for his compulsiveness to
express itself in action. The action is all predetermined and Musgrave
has to remain the embodiment of an idea, the voice of a conscience
which isn't his.

And of course the other soldiers have less individuality still.
They're there because Arden wants three soldiers to surround the
dominant figure of the Serjeant. The need to differentiate between
them was secondary and the choice of temperament for them was
fairly arbitrary – the Joking Soldier, the Surly Soldier and the Grey-
Haired Soldier.

In itself, of course, it doesn't matter how a playwright arrives at

John Arden

his end-product, so long as the end-product is satisfactory. What I find absolutely unsatisfactory about these three soldiers is the way they react to Annie in the stable. The scene is conceived like a ballad, with the girl offering herself to each of the three men in turn. This might have worked if the whole scene (and the whole play) were stylized in such a way as to make us accept the reactions of the three men in an unrealistic convention. But Arden writes the scene as if he believes that men like Hurst and Attercliffe really would react in this way.

> ANNIE (*with tender humour*): Here I come. Hello. I'm cold. I'm a blue ghost come to haunt you. Brrr. Come on, boy, warm me up. You'll not catch cold off *me*.
>
> HURST (*getting up*): No . . . I daresay not . . . (*They put their arms round each other.*)
> But what about the morning?
>
> ANNIE: Ah, the morning's different, ent it? I'll not say nowt about mornings, 'cos then we'll *all* be cold. Cold and alone. Like, stand in a crowd but every one alone. One thousand men makes a regiment, you'd say?
>
> HURST: Near enough.
>
> ANNIE: But for all that, when you're with them, you're still alone. Ent that right? So huggle me into the warm, boy, now. Keep out of the wind. It's late, Dark.
>
> HURST (*suddenly breaking away from her*): No, I won't. I don't care what I said afore, it's all done, ended, capped – get away. Go on. Leave me be.

And here is Attercliffe:

> ATTERCLIFFE: Now then, what'll I do to you, eh? How d'you reckon you're going to quench *me*? Good strong girly with a heart like a horse-collar, open it up and let 'em all in. And it still wouldn't do no good.
>
> ANNIE (*hard and hostile*): Wouldn't it? Try.
>
> ATTERCLIFFE: Ah, no. Not tonight. What would *you* know of soldiers?
>
> ANNIE: More'n you'd think I'd know, maybe.
>
> ATTERCLIFFE: I doubt it. Our Black Jack'd say it's not material. He'd say there's blood on these two hands. (*He looks at his hands with distaste*) You can wipe 'em as often as you want on a

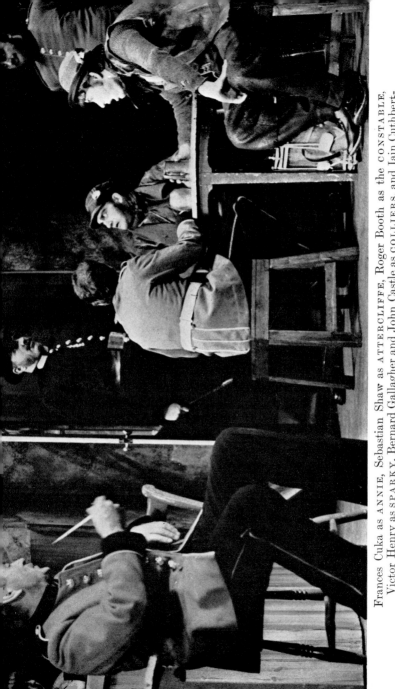

Frances Cuka as ANNIE, Sebastian Shaw as ATTERCLIFFE, Roger Booth as the CONSTABLE, Victor Henry as SPARKY, Bernard Gallagher and John Castle as COLLIERS, and Iain Cuthbertson as MUSGRAVE in the Royal Court production of *Serjeant Musgrave's Dance*.

Scene from the Chichester production of *The Workhouse Donkey* (1963).
Above: Alison Leggatt as LADY SWEETMAN, Martin Boddey as SIR
HAROLD, Anthony Nicholls as FENG, Dudley Foster as BOOCOCK and
Fay Compton as MRS BOOCOCK; Below: Michael Turner and Michael
Rothwell as STONE-MASONS with Frank Finlay as BUTTERTHWAITE.

bit o' yellow hair but it still comes blood the next time so why bother, *he'd* say. And *I'd* say it too. Here. (*He kisses her again and lets her go.*) There you are, girly: I've given you all you should get from a soldier. Say 'Thank you, boy', and that's that.

The writing in these passages, especially Attercliffe's dialogue, certainly has a power and a charm and a kind of poetry of its own, and this makes up for a lot, but Hurst's and Attercliffe's rejection of Annie have nothing at all to do with the mood or mental make-up of either of them. In fact it has nothing to do with particular experience at all – it's a reaction imposed on them in order to achieve an illustration of human experience in general. The morning is always different for everybody and the guilt feelings always survive for everybody. In making the two men reach their decision like this, Arden is transforming them into ballad characters.

But he doesn't use them consistently like this and he often makes them perpetrate actions which are meaningless unless they're linked up more deeply with intentions which imply more freedom of choice than the characters have. This is why the death of Sparky falls so flat. It's a key point in the action, the turning point in the relationship between the three surviving soldiers, and it ought to be an effective climax in itself, but in fact it has very little emotional impact. The reason is that the act of killing him is an action without an intention behind it. Or if the intention is there, it isn't brought into the picture. It is Hurst who kills Sparky by jumping on Attercliffe who has the bayonet in his hand, so that it goes into Sparky's stomach. But it's never made clear how deliberate the killing is, and in any case it doesn't correspond with any deeply felt intention on Hurst's part. Certainly, like Sailor Sawney, he's a 'killer' but, to make the act of killing theatrically meaningful, it isn't enough just to establish him as the type of man who kills, even though we know that he's irritated by Sparky and that he knows Sparky is planning to desert. The question of why Hurst kills Sparky is never seriously asked or answered. Arden goes along with Musgrave who says that it isn't material. It's just an incident that has its consquences later in the market-place scene when Annie uses it to discredit Musgrave and the others in front of the colliers.

It's because he's so uninterested in motivation that Arden manages
for so much of the time with such inarticulate characters. Except for
Sir David Lindsay in *Armstrong's Last Goodnight,* hardly any of his
protagonists can think or express themselves with any clarity. In
Live Like Pigs this doesn't damage the play at all because the main
point about the Sawneys is that they live by their instincts and that
their values are determined by a tradition which has nothing to do
with words or logic. But in *Serjeant Musgrave's Dance* it's very
damaging, because 'the Word' is so important to Musgrave.

> . . . take count of the corruption, then stand before this
> people with our white shining word, and let it dance! It's a hot
> coal, this town, despite that it's freezing – choose your minute
> and blow: and whoosh, she's flamed your roof off! They're
> trembling already into the strikers' riots. Well, their riots and
> our war are the same one corruption. This town is ours, it's
> ready for us: and its people, when they've heard us, and the
> Word of God, crying the murders that we've done – I'll tell
> you they'll turn to us, and they'll turn against that war!

To make him speak like this, lumping the strikers' riots and the
colonial wars together as part of the same corruption, is to make him
a mouthpiece for a rather incoherent socialist point of view that
blames both on the basic economic system. This would be all right
if we were meant to see him as a socialist and if he were put into focus
as such, but the play never brings his incoherent socialism into line
with his belief in the Logic of God's Word.

Even the references to madness aren't enough to resolve the
confusion because the madness isn't sufficiently put into perspective
either by the action or by the discussion in the play. Confusion is at
its worst in the crucial market-place scene in Act Three, where it
never becomes clear what it is that Musgrave is aiming for. Obviously
we're meant to feel sympathy with his condemnation of the war as
evil – and we do – but this sympathy becomes a source of extra
strain when his objectives seem to change from moment to moment.
At first it seems that he only wants to convince the crowd of the evils
of colonial war. He tells the story of how Billy Hicks was killed and
how five people were slaughtered to avenge him. Whether the

parallel with Cyprus is in our minds or not, the obvious injustice makes its point. Then he asks Walsh, as the most intelligent of the colliers, to give his opinion about the men who were responsible for the outrage. Next he seems to think that if he killed twenty-five people in the market-place (twenty-five being the same ratio to five that five is to one) this will put an end to the war that's still in progress and to war everywhere for all time. Then he asks who will help him, expecting Walsh to agree with him and with the idea of starting off the slaughter with the Mayor and the Parson, who have both made speeches urging the colliers to join the army. But when the aggressive Hurst is about to carry out Musgrave's threat and open fire on the crowd, Musgrave prevents him. Musgrave knows that the Grenadiers are coming, but he still hasn't done anything by the time they arrive.

This indecision could itself have made very good dramatic material if only it were shown up as such, but it never comes into focus properly. Arden must have been aware that his big scene hadn't resolved the confusion because he found it necessary to tack on another scene after the climax that ought to have ended the play. Mrs Hitchcock visits Musgrave and Attercliffe in prison, bringing a glass of port and lemon. But the discussion only succeeds in making points that have been made quite adequately already.

MRS HITCHCOCK: Listen: last evening you told all about this anarchy and where it came from – like, scribble all over with life or love, and that makes anarchy. Right?

MUSGRAVE: Go on.

MRS HITCHCOCK: Then *use* your Logic – if you can. Look at it this road: here we are, and we'd got life and love. Then you came in and you did your scribbling where nobody asked you. Aye, it's arsy-versey to what you said, but it's still an anarchy, isn't it? And it's all your own work.

MUSGRAVE: Don't tell me there was life or love in this town.

MRS HITCHCOCK: There was. There was hungry men, too – fighting for their food. But *you* brought in a different war.

MUSGRAVE: I brought it in to end it.

ATTERCLIFFE: To end it by its own rules: no bloody good. She's right, you're wrong. You can't cure the pox by further whoring. Sparky died of those damned rules. And so did the other one.

John Arden

Nothing at this stage could save the play because the confusion is right in the heart of it. It's a play in which Arden couldn't afford to ignore individuality and motivations in the way that he does. The areas within which the writing succeeds and the areas of failure can be clearly defined. It succeeds where the emphasis is on the group or on the social, political or economic background. It fails when individuals step into the foreground. The Mayor and the Parson are pathetically unconvincing in their big scenes because Arden is only interested in what they do, not at all in what they are. The Mayor is made to be the Unscrupulous Employer, the man who locks his labourers out and pretends that they're striking, the man who uses his public office for his private ends, carrying the Parson and the Constable with him on a tide of hypocrisy. In Lindsay Anderson's production, Richard Caldicot made a very good shot at the Parson, but these three parts are almost unplayable because the villainy is so trite and the irony so heavy-handed.

With the colliers, it's different. They don't stand out as individuals but most of the time they don't need to. Dramatically, they're at their most effective as members of a crowd in the pub or as dark, silent, threatening figures, with picks on their shoulders, looking suspiciously at the red-coated soldiers. Without saying a word, they sum up the unrest and victimization in the town, frozen in a movement, like people in a Lowry painting. Arden himself cites Lowry in the preface and the writing does capture this mood very well, particularly in the description of the town when the soldiers bring their reports to Musgrave in the churchyard.

> Coldest town I ever was in . . .
> Street empty, windows shut, two old wives on a doorstep go indoors the minute I come. Three men on one corner, two men on another, dirty looks and no words from any on 'em . . .
> Street empty, doors locked, windows blind, shops cold and empty. A young lass calls her kids in from playing in the dirt . . .
> Street empty, no chimneys smoking, no horses, yesterday's horsedung frozen on the road, Three men at a corner-post, four men leaning on a wall . . .

It's when the colliers have to speak out as individuals that the

28

writing sinks below this level. Here's a passage in which Walsh, the Earnest Collier, starts off talking very convincingly as a representative member of the group and goes on, not at all convincingly, as a mouthpiece for what Arden wants the play to say.

> EARNEST COLLIER: There's a Union made at this colliery, and we're strong. When we say strike, we strike, all ends of us: that's fists, and it's pick-hefts and it's stones and it's feet. If you work in the coal-seam you carry iron on your clogs – see! (*He thrusts up his foot menacingly.*)
> PUGNACIOUS COLLIER: And you fight for your life when it's needed.
> MUSGRAVE: So do some others of us.
> EARNEST COLLIER: Ah, no, lobster, *you* fight for pay. You go sailing on what they call punitive expeditions, against what you call rebels, and you shoot men down in streets.

It's very easy to sympathize with Arden's feelings and to respect him for thinking and caring more than most of us do about rebels shot down in streets, but it's difficult to accept this statement as coming from a collier, who surely couldn't be as aware as this about the punitive expeditions or talk like this about shooting men down in streets. Cyprus is casting too long a shadow here. It would be interesting to know more about how much anti-imperialist feeling there was in the unions at this time but Arden wasn't concerned to go into that or into the question of how Walsh came to be so well-informed.

The weaknesses of the play are the weaknesses of much of Arden's writing. The ballad tradition is useful when it enables characters to state simple emotions with a directness which might otherwise be difficult to take. But it's limiting when he has to deal with relationships and states of mind that aren't simple. Going back to the pools of common or archetypal experience that the ballads contain sometimes means going back to the cliché. And if so many of his characters get away with being inarticulate, it must mean that there's nothing he needs them to be articulate about. If they're not going to make decisions for themselves or to analyse their own experiences or their own thought processes, there's no point in giving them the mental equipment to do so. What Arden's characters so often do in prose is basically the same as what they do in verse when they're quoting or improvising songs and ballads – they're finding parallels between their own experience and the familiar experiences of the rhyme. So the cliché often determines the action, as it does with Attercliffe, when he says it's no use wiping bloody hands on a bit of yellow hair and *therefore* rejects Annie. When it isn't a cliché that determines the action, it's often the type that a character belongs to – and this is only another form of cliché. The Mayor is a corrupt capitalist and *therefore* behaves in the way that he does.

These are the limitations of Arden's method. They don't invalidate it. *Serjeant Musgrave's Dance* is still one of the best dozen plays to be written in England since the war. But it's too good a play for us to pretend that the weaknesses aren't there.

THE HAPPY HAVEN

Nothing Arden has written since *Live Like Pigs* and *Serjeant Musgrave's Dance* has been on the same level of achievement. But whether the later plays are failures or partial successes, they can't be dismissed. With his enormous energy and his wide-ranging imagination, Arden ventures into styles and periods where other Englishmen fear to tread. And if he fails, his failures are often more interesting than their stay-at-home successes.

The Happy Haven was written when Arden was at Bristol University for a year from 1959 to 1960 with a playwrighting fellowship. He had to write one play for performance in the drama studio, which is a converted squash court sometimes used for open stage productions and sometimes used as a lecture theatre. This must have made the passages in the play where the Doctor is lecturing to the audience much funnier and, as Arden has said: 'If you write a play for the open stage, it is by no means a foregone conclusion that it is going to have anything like the same effect when done in a conventional theatre.'

But the idea of using masks was in his mind before he went to Bristol. He first encountered them at the Royal Court Writers' Group, which used to meet once a week, under William Gaskill's direction, chiefly to do improvisations. One week George Devine came along to give a talk and a demonstration about Comic Masks. These are *commedia dell'arte* masks that cover the upper part of the face, except the eyes, leaving the mouth free. The actor puts one on, looks in a mirror and goes into an improvisation in the character that he sees himself to be. In some ways it's a very liberating sensation, because the mask dictates a clear and set outline for the character and the impossibility of going outside these limits gives you more freedom inside them.

After *Serjeant Musgrave's Dance*, in which the characters tend so much to be types rather than individuals, and in which their freedom of action is so circumscribed, it's not surprising that masks should appeal to Arden. Instead of soldiers who start off being called simply the Joking Soldier, the Surly Soldier and the Grey-Haired Soldier, acquiring names only in rehearsal, and colliers, only one of whom acquires a name, we have characters who stay all through the action in a mask that freezes the expression on their faces. Reviewing the play in *Encore,* Irving Wardle compared Arden's use of masks with his use of the ballad tradition.

> The components of the ballad include: boldness of gesture; formal repetition; impersonality and vigour of narrative; characterization by means of one or two hard details. All these clearly lend themselves to dramatic employment, and in *The Happy Haven* they are found in conjunction with Arden's own variant of the 'comedy of humours' which he develops to a logical conclusion by allotting to each character a mask representing such fixed attitudes as greed, frustrated motherhood, *bonhomie,* and arrested youth. The masks, besides defining the appropriate humour, also make the point that such attitudes are, literally, masks that have hardened with the years into a permanent shell over the natural features; and that when the doctor's elixir gives the wearers an opportunity to rip off their disguises they prefer to remain as they are.

This is one of the climaxes of the play – this rejection by the residents of the old people's home of the chance of being young again. If the play had been properly built up to lead to this point, it might have been an extremely interesting piece of writing. The trouble is that, as in *Serjeant Musgrave's Dance,* Arden keeps changing his focus and seems to keep changing his mind about what the play is about. Different kinds of comedy and different kinds of stylization pull the writing in different directions.

The Doctor comes off better than the patients. The part is played without a mask until the very end, when the patients turn the tables on him and rejuvenate him against his will. But the character is fiercely and effectively satirized in the writing. He's given the brisk, phoney conviviality that so many heads of institutions affect. His laboratory experiments, researching for the elixir, and his medical examinations of the patients are written on the level of pure farce, and when played at breakneck speed, as they were in William Gaskill's production with Peter Bowles as the Doctor, these scenes can be extremely funny.

> DOCTOR: Now don't you get flustered, Mr Golightly, old chap, about all this medical business, just a brief once-over, routine, routine. Had your X-rays taken? Hurry up with those – Robinson, X-rays, bring both lots in. Ah. Ninety-nine. One, two, three, *hup* – next one, one, two, three, *hup* good, good, waterworks, read the papers do you, good –
>
> HARDRADER: Doctor, I suppose –
>
> DOCTOR: Least said, soonest mended, that's the way, stiff upper lip – where are those X-rays?
>
> *(Orderly Robinson enters with two sets of X-rays.)*
>
> Let's have a look. *(Calls to upper stage.)* Mr Crape, please!
>
> *(Nurse Brown leads Crape off upper stage.)*
>
> Both sets, are they? Good. Nothing wrong here we can't set up with a couple of stitches. Right you are then, positive, positive – many happy years for the pair of you, eh? Don't you worry at all. That'll do, Nurse, take 'em away.
>
> *(Nurse Jones takes Golightly and Hardrader out as Nurse Brown brings in Crape at the same door, in his robe. Nurse Jones re-enters.)*
>
> X-rays taken, Mr Crape? Now this is just the usual medical business, no need to get flustered. Waterworks all right?

But this kind of fun doesn't really fit in with either the telephone conversation the Doctor has with the captain of his rugger team ('All right Charlie, I'll remember. I'll put 'em in the post for you. Medical goods, a plain envelope – *I* know the drill. We'll keep you a bachelor yet') or the one he has with his mother ('For God's sake let me invite my own girls to tea'). These might have served a purpose in showing us there was another side to the character, if it had been written in a different way but, as it is, the fact that Arden thought them necessary seems to suggest that he was expecting us to be taking the Doctor far more seriously than we possibly could be.

Nor does his treatment of the Doctor dovetail at all well with his treatment of the patients. They're simplified in an altogether different way. The quality that comes very clearly into focus is the childishness of the very old. We see one of them telling tales to the Doctor about the others, two of them playing games and cheating, one trying

to swindle money out of the other and all of them indulging in
fantasies, some about love, some about power. Events like having
tea and having a bath take on enormous importance. At first all this
is funny and effective, but the details soon come to be laid on rather
too thickly. Crape, the telltale, who's a direct descendant of Joe
Parker and the Bargee, has a rhyme that he sings to himself:

> The darkening age of James J. Crape
> Yet burns with one surviving fire:
> To see the old fools all a-shiver and a-quiver
> At the secret probings of my power!

And altogether there are too many points like this where the presen-
tation of naïvety strikes us as being itself far too naïve.

Part of Arden's purpose, it seems, is to stop us from identifying
with the old people. He could have trusted the masks to do this
without making the people themselves quite so silly. They're all
taken in very easily, as Golightly is, singing his 'melancholy song' to
Mrs Phineus while she polishes off the tea that's been brought for both
of them.

> The life of man is lost and lonely,
> Whereas the porpoise and the whale
> They both have meaning and conclusion –
> (*The song loses coherence.*)
> But he finds no meaning nor conclusion
> He finds no meaning nor –
> Whereas the porpoise and the whale –
> I don't believe it! have always said love, Mrs Phineus, I have
> always believed it, I must still believe it, you cannot but credit
> that I have always certainly held to it, and even if without true
> experience, look, I have never really been able to put it to the
> proof – oh my dear, dear Mrs Phineus, I have never killed a
> whale, I have never *seen* a whale, nor yet travelled on a ship,
> except to the Isle of Wight when my sister lived in Shanklin –
> but, Love, it must surely be Love, *there* is a star that will not
> turn, I have had faith in this, for years, years, please, it must
> be true, *Love* is the meaning, say it is the conclusion – say it say it
> – *please!* . . . Why, you've finished up all the tea, Mrs Phineus.
> PHINEUS: Oh no, not all of it. Surely not.

GOLIGHTLY: But then, I suppose, I suppose why not? Is it not your prerogative? Indeed, dear lady, are you not fully entitled – perhaps there is just a little bit left at the bottom of the pot? Oh dear, oh dear. Well then . . . And after all she brought very few sandwiches, and small ones, small . . . Perhaps I may have eaten one without actually noticing? I *do* feel quite full, as though I *had* had tea. I am quite absent-minded. Yes.

What works best in the writing is the direct statement of very simple feelings, as in this speech of Mrs Phineus's.

> I'm an old old lady
> And I don't have long to live.
> I am only strong enough to take
> Not to give. No time left to give.
> I want to drink, I want to eat.
> I want my shoes taken off my feet.
> I want to talk but not to walk
> Because if I walk, I have to know
> Where it is I want to go.
> I want to sleep but not to dream
> I want to play and win every game
> To live with love but not to love
> The world to move but me not move
> I want I want for ever and ever.
> The world to work, the world to be clever.
> Leave me be, but don't leave me alone.
> That's that I want. I'm a big round stone
> Sitting in the middle of a thunderstorm.

The simplification in the writing and the simplicity of the characters go together, but neither goes with the seriousness of some of the conversations about old age or with the scene when the characters decide to turn down the chance of becoming young again. Coming from them, the decision doesn't amount to very much. They aren't real enough or complex enough or interesting enough. It's all too obvious that their lives wouldn't be worth having all over again, even to them.

CRAPE: Old chap. Old chap Hardrader. Big strong games and sports, boxing and cricket, badminton and the high-jump,

John Arden

Egyptian P.T. Only two friends and one of them's in her grave – you couldn't make her love you, so you went toughing it on the greensward and bellowing at your dirty dog. If you were to start again, what would *you* find?

HARDRADER: I hope I would find a healthy humane existence.

GOLIGHTLY: No no, excuse me, no: Mr Hardrader. You would be as lonely as ever you were. I know, because *I* would be, too. Isn't it terrifying?

CRAPE: Isn't it?

Crape persuades Mrs Phineus that she doesn't want to go back to the discomforts and messiness of being a baby all over again. Golightly's chief reason for wanting to be young again had been to marry Mrs Phineus and Crape doesn't let him get away with the argument that there are plenty of others. 'There always were plenty of others,' he retorts. 'How many of them did you get?' And Mrs Letouzel rejects the chance out of the same fear of loneliness as Mr Hardrader. Crape makes her confess that there never was a Mr Letouzel and she makes Crape confess that he's enjoying puncturing everybody's fantasies. It's a Pirandello scene in a very un–Pirandello play, which is far more effective when it gets back to the stylized comedy at the end. It's like *Serjeant Musgrave's Dance* in that the climax of the argument comes separately from the climax of the action, but this time the climax of action comes last. Having decided that they don't want the elixir, the patients rebel against the Doctor and expose him in front of a bevy of distinguished visitors. Hardrader holds the Doctor, Mrs Letouzel pulls his trousers down and Mrs Phineus produces an enormous hypodermic from her bag which she sticks into his bottom. He goes off-stage to reappear in a childish mask and short trousers. The old people chase out the visitors and for once the forces of anarchy have won.

THE BUSINESS OF GOOD
GOVERNMENT

The Business of Good Government is a nativity play that Arden wrote
for performance in the village church of Brent Knoll in Somerset.
It's an experiment in yet another different style but it returns to the
political theme which has been almost missing from *The Happy
Haven,* in which the only reference to politics comes in a conversation
between Crape and Mrs Letouzel in Act One when they talk about
a Bounty paid by the Ministry of Health. The subject is introduced
as though it's going to be developed, but it's dropped. In *The
Business of Good Government,* however, immediately after the introductory carol, the dialogue constructs a firm bridge between religion
and politics. Following the Angel's declaration from the pulpit.

> Behold, I bring you tidings of great joy, which shall be unto all
> people. Glory to God in the highest, and on earth peace, good-
> will towards men.

Herod's reply is:

> Goodwill, great joy, peace upon earth – I do not believe they
> are altogether possible. But it is the business of good govern-
> ment to try and make them possible.

This also establishes an immediate contact between the two kinds of
language: the exalted, biblical language of the Angel, and the modern,
colloquial language of Herod. And throughout the play, we have a
great refinement on the technique we first met in *Soldier, Soldier* of
using different styles of language for different grades of character.
Herod puts an immediate and witty focus on his political and
economic problems.

> To the west, the Roman Empire. To the east, the Persian
> Empire. In the middle, a small country in a very dangerous
> position. If I lean towards the east, I am afraid of invasion
> from Rome: if I lean towards Rome, then I shall be called upon

to fight Persia. I would prefer to choose neither. But I had to choose Rome, because Rome rules Egypt, and it is from Egypt that we buy our corn. We are not self-supporting. *I* am not self-supporting. I have Roman officers in my army, Roman advisers in my palace, Roman spies in every department of state . . .

(*The Secretary rises from his seat and moves towards Herod. He notices this and immediately changes his tone to one of insincere political rhetoric.*)

The enormous friendship and generosity shown by the Roman people to the people of Judaea can only be repaid by our continued loyalty and vigilance.

The parallels with contemporary power politics are impossible to miss. It's a curious view of Herod, who isn't usually thought of in terms of the difficulties he had in governing Judaea, but Arden sustains this successfully through the play. Even when he's about to order the massacre, his speech is a deliberate echo of Macmillan's 'You've never had it so good'.

Citizens! Patriots! Through the years I have been your leader I have kept you free from war and provided unexampled prosperity. You are richer and happier than ever you have been! Your children are receiving opportunities for education and advancement that your own fathers could not have imagined in their wildest dreams. Dare you see this prosperity destroyed in one night? You answer me – no.

Arden extracts a good deal of unlikely comedy from the subject. His Shepherds are a bit anaemic compared with those in some of the Mystery Plays, but he uses the Three Wise Men for some pleasant satire on diplomatic protocol and he keeps a light touch, avoiding sentiment and conventionality when they present their gifts to the Child. The Landlady is rather reminiscent of the one in *Serjeant Musgrave's Dance* with her complaints about billeting and having to give credit to the government, and the Midwife is given an amusing, modern, middle-class fussiness when she tells the Shepherds off for breathing too close to the Child and making too much noise with their boots. The play moves easily and informally between the different scenes, the different settings and the different groups of characters.

The Business of Good Government

Most of the characters are in full view of the audience most of the time, with the Angel in the pulpit, sometimes helping to link the scenes together and sometimes used as a kind of prompter, joining in the conversations of the Three Wise Men, although they don't see him, so that the effect is as if he's planting thoughts in their consciousnesses.

BLACK WISE MAN (*quickly*): Do you think –
OLD WISE MAN: I think –
ANGEL: I think you would be best advised
YOUNG WISE MAN: I think we would be best advised to leave the country quietly and forget the whole business.
BLACK WISE MAN: Yes, very true: I think that *is* wisest.
ANGEL: You had better go home.
OLD WISE MAN (*hurrying down from the stage*): We had better go home!

In this section, the Angel is coming down to the prose level of the Three Wise Men. After the birth, Joseph and Mary rise to the higher level of the Angel's speech and all three speak in verse. The writing succeeds in taking all these transitions into its stride.

If the end strikes us as unsatisfactory, it may be partly because the play was written for a particular occasion, not for a particular purpose. It's disappointing that Arden doesn't manage to make more of the relationship he starts between the religious theme and the political theme. It might have been better if the focus had stayed as it was at the beginning and we'd seen more of the pressures that drove Herod to order the massacre, but it's shifted, as so often in Arden, and we don't see into his mind at this point. Theatrically, the massacre is realized quite effectively in a stylized way with a clash of cymbals and wailing heard in different places all over the hall. But the end is very inconclusive. Joseph, Mary and the Child escape safely into Egypt thanks to a miracle that makes a field of corn grow as fast in an hour as it would normally grow in three months. This prevents Herod from pursuing when the Farm-Girl tells him that she was sowing the field when a man and woman passed with a young child. After this, all that happens is that the actors line up singing the Corpus Christi Carol and go out in procession, still singing.

WET FISH

Wet Fish, a play for television, was transmitted in September 1961. It is the most straightforward and the least distinctive of any of Arden's plays to date. The plotting is complex and competent, and though the story is a little slow to get under way, it moves to an effective climax.

It revives Krank from *The Waters of Babylon* while Teresa and Butterthwaite figure as off-stage characters. It also introduces Sir Harold Sweetman, a character who is to reappear in *The Workhouse Donkey.*

If Krank seems less explosive and less expansive than when we last saw him, it's partly because the style of the writing is more reserved and naturalistic, partly because his share of the action is smaller, and partly because we see him chiefly in the architect's office, where a lot of the play is set. Krank is working for Gilbert Garnish, a brisk Yorkshireman who started small but now runs a large, busy, highly successful firm. His first client, twenty-three years ago, was a fishmonger, Treddlehoyle, who's still in the same open-fronted shop that Garnish designed for him, though now he wants some alterations done to it. Garnish puts Ruth Parsons on the job, an assistant who's never handled a job before on her own. He gives the contract to a builder called Barker, partly because Barker's brother is going to be Chairman of the City Housing Committee and Garnish wants to use him to pull strings to get a big redevelopment scheme under way.

There are scenes which show in detail the building work being done in the fish shop and the chaos which it causes to the business. Garnish has to spend a lot of time in Paris and leaves everything to Ruth, who gets into a mess and has to send out a lot of Variation Orders, bumping up the cost of the job. Garnish has told her to consult his chief assistant if she gets into difficulties, but, like all the women in *The Waters of Babylon,* she lets herself be seduced by Krank, who tells her that she and he will do it between them.

Arden shows his usual interest in the manœuvrings of local

Albert Finney as GILNOCKIE in the Chichester production of *Armstrong's Last Goodnight*.

Last Scene from *Armstrong's Last Goodnight* with Albert Finney.

politics. Garnish has lunch with Barker's brother and Alderman Butterthwaite and, as a result of this, the Planning Committee decides to go ahead with the Prince Consort Street development, with Garnish as architect and Barker as builder. Meanwhile the Local Authority's Building Inspector orders that the whole roof of the fish shop building must be pulled down and rebuilt. Treddlehoyle is infuriated by this and by the fact that Garnish isn't doing more of the work himself. The growing friction between the two men is very convenient for Krank, who has bought the neighbouring houses on either side of the fish shop. When Treddlehoyle gets out of his financial depth, Krank offers to buy his house from him, rent him the shop and pay for all the work that has to be done. Treddlehoyle quarrels with Garnish, barging in on a lunch he's having with Archdeacon Pole-Hatchett and Sir Harold Sweetman. This is a very good scene in which the indignation of the little man produces considerable embarrassment to the local bigwigs, and the action moves quickly from this climax to the effective downbeat ending, when Treddlehoyle decides to take the work out of Garnish's hands and give it to Krank, in whom his young and attractive wife feels so much confidence.

It's not an important play, but it succeeds within the terms that it sets itself. The architect's office and the fish shop are both brought to life in considerable detail. Krank's business side-lines don't obtrude much on the action and the municipal jiggery-pokery is worked out much more convincingly than in any of the stage plays, partly, perhaps, because we don't see the protagonists or the meetings at which the decisions are taken: we only hear about them at second hand. The dialogue lacks the flashes of poetry and brilliance that illuminate it in some of the other plays, but it's realistic, consistent and always lively. It's interesting to see Arden bringing off such a degree of workmanlike success within such a naturalistic framework.

IRONHAND

Ironhand is Arden's translation of Goethe's *Goetz von Berlichingen mit der eisernen Hand.* It was optioned by Peter Hall but never produced until Val May put it on at the Bristol Old Vic in November 1963. Like Goethe's original, and like Sartre's play about Goetz, *Le Diable et le Bon Dieu,* it has yet to be seen in London.

It is not an attempt at a literal translation. Arden has done a great deal to tidy up Goethe's sprawling construction, making five acts into three, changing the running order of some of the scenes, usually for the better, telescoping scenes together, cutting down on the soliloquies and substituting illustrative incidents for expository statements wherever possible. But he hasn't changed the character of Weislingen as much as he seems to think he has, judging from his introductory note, and he hasn't really made the resulting picture of Goetz any more balanced that it is in Goethe. Certainly it is quite unrealistic to say, as John Russell Taylor does in *Anger and After,* 'Where Goethe could bring himself to show only one side fairly, Arden again states all sides of the case with equal care and justice.' In fact Goethe uses Weislingen to put the case against Goetz very clearly. But, apart from a few rather distracting north-countryisms – not only in the peasants' speeches, but in Goetz's – Arden captures the flavour of the original very well.

I think it is a mistake to make Goethe's Brother Martin into Martin Luther. Part of the point of the scene is that Goethe's monk recognizes Goetz as being a great man; there is no question of his being a great man himself – he has all the attributes of the small man. On the other hand, Arden does serve the play well by writing in build-ups for which the twenty-four-year-old Goethe, in his headlong imitation of Shakespeare's epic method, didn't have the time or the technique. The session of the secret tribunal, for instance, in Act Three is all the more effective for the fact that Arden has planted a reference to secret tribunals in the Bishop's dinner party scene in Act One.

Unfortunately, though, Arden does not limit himself to the explanations that are necessary. He lengthens a lot of the big speeches, making them far too explicit in the process. Goethe himself often overwrote, and Arden certainly cuts down on the romantic rhetoric, but he introduces a new rhetoric of explanatory recapitulation. Goetz's dying speech is a case in point. In Goethe, he dies just after Elisabeth, his wife, tells him that Georg, his page, has died fighting.

> Thank God! He was the best boy under the sun, and brave. – Let my soul go now. – Poor woman! I am leaving you in a ruined world. Lerse, stay with her. Keep your hearts shut like gates. An age of deceit is on its way. The unworthy will govern with guile, and the noble will fall into their nets. Maria, may God give you back your husband! May he not fall so low as he has risen high! He died and the good Emperor died and my Georg. – Give me a glass of water. – Heavenly air! – Liberty! Liberty! (*He dies.*)

In Arden's play, Georg doesn't die fighting but gets hanged by Weislingen's men at Miltenberg. Goetz asks whether he was hanged from a tree or a gallows.

LERSE: What difference does it make?
GOETZ: I hope it was a tree. He was a free robber's man and he should die in the green forest. Here is where *I* die, between these great stones. Eh, not entirely, you will tell me. They let me sit in this garden; it has one little bush. . . So am I, do you see, one little bush, and I was born a tall tree in the middle of a free forest. Weislingen told me I did not know what freedom was. He said it was not possible for me to be free when I inhibited the freedom of other good men. I told him they were treacherous. The peasants were treacherous because they burnt down Miltenberg when they swore they would not. Yet I believed in their cause. All they did was fight for it in the only way they knew. If we all fought for our causes we should all fight each other . . . Where's that mercenary man? *You* would fight for anybody if they gave you the pay or a promise of good bloodshed – open your eyes, man, you should have asked them all why, you should know *why* you are fighting! Or else we are just wild animals, we must be shut up in boxes and that's where I am. Because I stood by myself and I took no heed of nobody. All I said was freedom: all Weislingen said was some sort of order. To put the two together: all the world is broken

43

John Arden

up, and yet we must break it and break it and break it . . . Oh
God, I am not strong enough – I don't think there's anyone
can call himself strong enough – and yet it has to be done . . .
After I am dead, should I expect my freedom then? But I inhibited the freedom of other good men and gave them no
order. So what do I deserve? . . . By God's feet I will tell you. I
deserve my true freedom and so do they all! And we deserve to
be told what are the true questions and what are the answers,
and we deserve to be able to tell them to our sons! And all that
is impossible . . . You will break yourselves up, you will turn
upside-down, you will destroy yourselves with it – there is
always one possibility, that one day you will find it. You are
made not to rest until you have found it. Freedom. And no
warfare. Freedom. And good order. Freedom. (*He falls back in
his chair.*)

I have quoted this at length because it not only provides a good
example of how the overwriting differs from Goethe's, but it also
acts as a good pointer to what it was in the play that attracted Arden
so much. The impossibility of finding the right combination of liberty
and order has been one of the main themes in everything he has
written, and in *Goetz*, as in so many of his plays, the anarchy is
attractive but anachronistic. The forces of progress are on the side
of the centralism that mops up the pockets of individual freedom and
resistance as it spreads its organizing power, whether it is centralism
in a modern English town, as in *Live Like Pigs*, or imperialism in
sixeenth-century Germany. And Goetz is the perfect robber-baron
figure: the hereditary lord who gets chosen by the rebellious peasants
as their leader, the aristocratic champion of democracy, the good
man who puts himself outside the law, while villains like Weislingen
go on enjoying the favours of their Emperor.

These themes all correspond to themes Arden had handled before;
what is more important is to see how Goethe left his mark on everything Arden went on to write afterwards. *The Workhouse Donkey,
Armstrong's Last Goodnight* and *Left-Handed Liberty* show how important *Ironhand* was as a watershed in his development. It is not
only that he has been influenced in the way he handles the themes –
he is influenced by the size of the conception. Having once worked on
an epic scale, even as a translator, he has never since reduced the

size of his canvas to what it was in *Live Like Pigs* or *The Happy Haven*. Of course, this is only another way of saying that Goethe sent him back to Shakespeare. *The Workhouse Donkey*, with a north-country town councillor cast in the role of a robber baron, may make us think of Goethe before we think of Shakespeare, but Shakespeare is there in the background. The polarity between order and anarchy was a theme that obsessed him too: Falstaff and Hotspur are aligned against the old King and the Lord Chief Justice in very much the same way, with Hal in the middle having to choose.

Arden was already developing into being the most Shakespearean of contemporary English playwrights. Goethe helped him on his way.

THE WORKHOUSE DONKEY

The Workhouse Donkey was commissioned by the Royal Court but first performed at Chichester in July 1963.

There's a lot of bad blank verse in it and none of Arden's best writing, except for one good song which comes at the weakest point in the action. It's a cumbersome play but it's conceived on a big scale and it's his most wholehearted attempt to give a full picture of a local borough as a kind of modern city-state. The town is presented as practically self-governing and it is the business of good government which is our main subject. There's one group representing the Labour councillors, who are in power, and one group representing the Conservatives. The police figure even more prominently than usual in Arden's work, with four policemen and one ex-policeman in the cast. Much of the action centres on the appointment of a new chief of police, Colonel Feng, and the attempts of both political factions to get him on their side or to get rid of him for being on the other side. The ordinary electorate is represented by a corrupt doctor, his attractive daughter, and the manageress of a local night-club owned by Sir Harold Sweetman, who now figures as the leader of the Conservatives. The only social element missing from the picture – and it's a curious omission – is the working classes.

The plot is extremely complex but the basic conflict is between Colonel Feng and Charlie Butterthwaite. Feng is a man of unshakable integrity, austere and fanatical, like Musgrave, but moral in his outlook; while Butterthwaite, the power behind the mayoral throne, is much more likeable but quite unscrupulous. He's always playing for popularity, peppering his speeches with jokes against himself and never missing a chance to make a joke or a speech. He practises a vulgar, back-slapping *bonhomie* which is often very irritating – not only to the other characters. But his vitality compensates for this. Like the Sawneys and Gilnockie, he's too big for the social framework that he has to live in, and like them, he's an anachronism. He's an old Socialist and still speaks nostalgically of the party's heroic infancy and his own skirmishes with the police. But his rebel spirit refuses to be confined under the alderman's gown. He ends up robbing the safe in the Town Hall and after that his career is finished. But in spite of everything, we're sorry when he goes.

Feng also gets himself into trouble. He falls in love with the doctor's daughter and feels he has to protect her father, who was an accomplice in Butterthwaite's crime. But when Feng loses his job, Arden doesn't make us feel so much for him.

One of the oddities of the play is that while the intrigues that go on are extremely complex, some of the characters' motivations and some of their reactions are extremely simplified, as in *The Happy Haven* or as in a Brechtian fable, but without being stylized in anything like the same way – or anything like enough to justify the simplification. Such stylization as there is often fails to work, as in this impersonal treatment of a highly personal moment between Feng and Wellesley, Dr Blomax's daughter.

> WELLESLEY: Oh, I'm so glad I didn't go to school here. I've got my father to thank for that if for nothing else. The day that you leave school here you're expected to reach the age of forty in about three hours and that's all. If you won't do it, you know what you get? Hump of the old shoulders and the old grunt comes out at you!
>
> > Too young, too tall, and your eyes too bright,
> > You look too near and you look too hard,
> > You dream too deep in the deep of the night,
> > And you walk too long in my backyard.
> > You stand and ask for your white bread
> > And you stand and you ask for your brown,
> > But what you will get is a good horse whip
> > To drive you out of town.
>
> How old are you, as a matter of interest?
>
> FENG: Oh? Oh, sufficiently old. No longer irresponsible. Rigid, you might say. Hardened arteries, young lady, unsympathetic and crumbling. Hardness, however, is nothing if not necessary. It derives from my post and my years in the Colonial Service and the necessity therein for unwavering powers of decision. And so I *have* decided. Quite suddenly. Unexpectedly. I am, alone, not sufficient, in fact I am bewildered. Particularly now, surrounded as I am by a confusion of democracy and alien loyalties, for support I turn – where? Of necessity to another

> alien. I would like you to become my wife . . . Or do you not
> perhaps share my belief in the similarity of our predicaments?
> I have within me – I mean as a man, not a policeman – an
> extraordinary humanity, of necessity concealed. Improbable
> longings, attempts at self-betrayal, I think I can crush
> them, by this improbable method. I would be glad of your
> opinion.

I don't think any director or any actor could make this passage work
properly for an audience, although the points that Arden is
trying to make in it are very well worth making. He's trying
to cut through the characters to an analysis of the pressures that
make them behave as they do and at the same time he's enjoying
the comedy that he gets out of the disparity between the two of
them, a disparity which makes Feng all the more nervous and
pedantic. Wellesley's ballad, which is perfunctorily tailored into its
context, is rather facile but Feng's analysis of his own situation
simplifies what it says in more or less the same way. Of course,
another of the points that Arden is trying to make is that this is
basically how decisions get taken. This may be true but in practice
we aren't convinced.

The most implausible moment of all comes when Butterthwaite
burgles the safe. Like Krank in *The Waters of Babylon,* he is being
pressured to pay a debt of £500 – even the amount is the same – and
the reaction to the pressure is just as unconvincing. The method of
robbery is different but in both cases there's an attempt to steal from
the public purse. The ramifying repercussions of the theft in *The Workhouse Donkey* are worked out with great ingenuity but the damage to
the play isn't compensated by this or by the very good, rather
Brechtian song Butterthwaite has during the stealing, with inter-
ruptions between each verse.

> BUTTERTHWAITE: . . . There's nigh on a thousand in here. I
> don't know how many times I've had to tell those skiving
> clerks this is *not* the Barclays Bank!
>
> BLOMAX: But surely they'll have made a note of the num-
> bers?
>
> BUTTERTHWAITE: Not on your life they haven't! Ho, there's
> some head going to roll in this office tomorrow morning. (*He is*

counting out packets of banknotes.) There's your five hundred.
Put it in your pocket! Go on, put it in!

(*He sings*)

I thanked my benefactors thus
Hee-haw hee-haw haw.
I could not understand, you see,
Just how it was they thought of me
Or what it was they saw!

What am I going to do wi' t'rest? I might keep it. But I
won't. It'll only draw attention . . . I know . . .

(*He sings, and as he does so he scatters money about the stage.*)

I travelled out into that world
With never a backward glance,
The street was full of folk, they said,
He's got two ears upon his head
He's got four feet upon his legs
He's got . . . My God, look what he's got,
They cried, Get back to France!

I said, what do you mean, France? I've never been to France
in my life! I wor born in the workhouse. I never set foot over
the doorstone while this morning!

They cried, Get back to France!
Oh my God, it makes me tired . . .

I could not think what I had done
That I was so derided
For Nature gives no donkey less
Than what I was provided.

You see what I'm doing? We scatter it around, thereby indi-
cating a similitude of ludicrous panic . . . as though disturbed
in the act we have fled from the scene in terrified disorder.

I said – hee-haw – you're very rude
I do the best I can.
You couldn't treat me worse, I said,
If I was a human man!

Arden has to use Procrustean methods to make the plot work.
The meetings of the councillors are realistically written, though they
go into many boring and unnecessary details. And scenes like the
police check on the pub after closing time and the police raid on the
night-club are worked out very well. As in *Serjeant Musgrave's Dance,*

John Arden

the ensemble scenes are the best. But, as with the Mayor and the Parson in *Musgrave,* the corruption of the doctor seems slightly shallow and the relationship between the corrupt Sir Harold Sweetman and the corrupt Superintendent Wiper isn't made very plausible. Sweetman has been paying him to protect the club but when Butterthwaite lays information against it, Wiper goes to consult Sweetman because he's worried it will come out that Gloria, the manageress, was tipped off in advance about the police raid. This is acceptable enough, but the conversation between the two men falls half-way between social satire and board-room thriller.

SWEETMAN: Then we'd better tell the Chief Constable. (*He goes towards the telephone.*) No. Wait. Have they been charged? I mean, for drunkenness, or the like?

WIPER: Not yet, no . . .

SWEETMAN: Then see that they are not. The accusations they have brought are, ha-hm, very wild indeed, and we are in considerable danger here of a first-class political row. Men of that type who have been in absolute power for over thirty years, why, they'd stick at nothing. We don't want to see a responsible public servant like Colonel Feng turned into a political shuttlecock. Do we? Get hold of all the other customers who were in the club this evening and get sworn affidavits as to the innocence of the show, and also, if you like, the hooliganism of Butterthwaite. Impress Colonel Feng with the hooliganism of Butterthwaite.

WIPER: What about the club itself?

SWEETMAN: Yes . . . I'll have to think of something. I may turn it to advantage . . . Yes. Good night, Superintendent.

Most of the scenes of machination work well enough theatrically, though there are too many of them, but the level of the writing sags badly whenever characters are left with a chink of freedom to make their own minds up. Then they're liable to fall into simplifications like Feng's in the scene with Wellesley or into soliloquies like this one of Blomax's. He's been hobnobbing with Butterthwaite and the Socialists, which annoys the Sweetmans, whose son wants to marry Wellesley. Gloria, who's now married to Blomax, wants to get

Butterthwaite out of the way because he's becoming too much of a
threat to the survival of the club.

GLORIA: We want an answer from you before you go to bed.
BLOMAX: Bed?
GLORIA: Aye, bed …
     And the shape of your answer
     Will doubtless decide
     Whether that bed
     Will be narrow or wide! – hubby!
     (*She goes into the house.*)
BLOMAX: Well, whether it's one or whether it's the other, I still
    seem to have invited into it the east wind and the west and
    they're scrapping like two catamounts between my skin and my
    pyjamas …
     *(He picks up the empty bottles, pours out the dregs into one
    bottle, and drinks it.)*
    Fact of the matter is, I *have* been betraying my class. Wellesley
    is entitled to the natural advantages of her place in society,
    the snooty little bitch. I am, after all, a comfortable man: and
    I don't want to be disrupted. When all is said and done,
    this town is run by an ignorant overweening yobbo: and it's
    time I stood up firm to him and accepted the responsibilities
    of my superior education . . . Furthermore, he owes me
    money.

The major success of the play is the creation of the character of
Butterthwaite. He's glib, transparent and tiresome, but he's big. In
fact he's something of a Dickensian character. Arden himself has
drawn attention to a nineteenth-century element in the play. In an
interview he gave to *Plays and Players* (August 1963) he made the
point that towns like Wakefield or Pudsey or Barnsley have a nineteenth-century atmosphere.

> … they're run by councillors who are mostly elderly men; the
> Labour Parties are pretty conservative up there; they've been
> based on a kind of Trade Union backing, and there's also a pretty
> strong non-conformist attitude to life, and it's all a sort of hang-
> over from the nineteenth century . . . and of course I am in-
> fluenced by the nineteenth century theatre to some extent; I
> don't mean so much the plays as the approach to the theatre, the

> type of staging, the strong lines of character drawing and plot that
> were involved, you know; they didn't go in much for subtle
> playmaking and I think that I'm very much influenced by that. I
> have one of these nineteenth century toy theatres which I enjoy
> playing with, and I think that there is a certain element of this
> in my writing.

And in an interview he gave to Stuart Burge on *Woman's Hour*, he
said that newspapers were an important source of material for him
in writing a play with a contemporary setting, particularly in *The
Workhouse Donkey*:

> I mingled in that comedy a great many real-life episodes and
> jumbled them up and fitted them into a plot, telescoping them.
> But there's hardly a scene in that play which hasn't got some
> source in the local newspapers of the North of England over the
> past ten years.

ARS LONGA, VITA BREVIS

Ars Longa, Vita Brevis is a very short play which was performed in
Peter Brook's Theatre of Cruelty at the LAMDA Theatre in January
1964.

It is a play about discipline taken to a grotesque extreme, with
grotesque characters who are rather reminiscent of the Doctor in
The Happy Haven in their manner of speaking.

> HEADMASTER: Mr Miltiades, how do you do? I hope you are,
> yes, very satisfactory references, and are you married?
> Married? I always like to think a teacher is married. Gives him
> a backbone or even a root. Ideas? Your ideas? What are they?
>
> ART-MASTER: Ideas, headmaster?
>
> HEADMASTER: Yes, your intentions, programme of work, views
> upon education, curriculum?
>
> ART-MASTER: No free expression.
>
> HEADMASTER: None?
>
> ART-MASTER: Not to start with. Highly perilous. Undesirable.
> Loosens, weakens, disintegrates, softens the foundations,
> carries away the moral fibre, shreds it, unravels it, scatters
> it abroad.

In his first art lesson the new master insists on absolute realism,
absolute precision and 4H pencils. Finding that some of the children
don't know their left hand from their right, he starts giving them drill
movements to do and marching them round the classroom. And from
that is is only one step to military exercises. He makes them stage the
killing of King Arthur at the battle of Camlann.

> Met by pikemen, on foot, stand firm, push of pike against broad-
> sword and shield. Push back parry shove heave kick thrust
> thump bang wallop hit knock topple 'em over. Where is
> Arthur? Where is Mordred? Stand forward, the two enemies,
> hate each other, deadly, poison, murder, you have stolen his
> wife and stolen his kingdom. You meet in the mellay. You
> don't know what a mellay is? I'll make you a mellay. Here you
> are, I've made it. Lost an eye, lost a tooth, lost a foot, lost a
> lung, that's as it should be, this is a battle. You recognize one

John Arden

another. Uncle against nephew. Honour against treason. Order against chaos. Kill each other kill each other kill each other KILL!

Going home to his wife, whose name is Roxana, the art-master, whose name is Antiochus, quarrels with her:

> Had I not married you, I would have enlisted as a soldier, I would have submitted myself to the glories of discipline and the beautiful discomforts of khaki serge, I would have enjoyed the manly companionship of the barrack room, the glowing brutalities of non-commissioned officers, and the rigours and delightful hardihood of the early morning drill parade. Art has failed me. Education has failed me. Marriage has failed me. Life has failed me. The world is unlaced, Roxana, unlaced, unbraced and falling apart, at every buttonhole. We must preserve rigidity, we must remember that unless we can subordinate ourselves wholeheartedly to the enthusiasm of total control we shall disintegrate.

He joins the Territorial Army and in an exercise they do in the woods, he has to dress up as a tree. The headmaster and the govenors of the school come into the woods to shoot and the headmaster kills the art-master, pretending to think that he is a deer. Dying, the art-master breaks into verse, as Krank did.

> Technology is confounded and art takes its place:
> For here I have received a real bullet in my face.
> Hardihood and discipline,
> Straight lines and repression
> Have today found their old true expression

The govenors raise a subscription for the widow and the headmaster gives it to her.

WIFE: Thank you so very much. Now I can have all those things that I was unable to enjoy because of the poor pay of the teaching profession.

HEADMASTER: With the money she buys clothes, food, wine, a new house, and she enjoys herself in fast cars with innumerable young men, all more handsome and less confused than her late husband. In the middle of her enjoyment she meets his funeral on the way to the graveyard.

54

WIFE: I shed a tear upon his bier
    Because to me he was ever dear
    But I could not follow him in all his wishes
    I prefer the quick easy swimming of the fishes
    Which sport and play
    In green water all day
    And have not a straight line in the whole of their bodies.

Once again this is a departure into a completely new style for Arden, moving much closer to the Theatre of the Absurd than ever before, and working without the simplification that bedevils *The Happy Haven*. The language is compact and witty and a vast amount of narrative space is covered in very little time.

A'RMSTRONG'S LAST GOODNIGHT

Armstrong's Last Goodnight was premiered at the Glasgow Citizen's Theatre in May 1964, in a production by Dennis Carey with Iain Cuthbertson as Gilnockie. It was revived in 1965 at the Chichester Festival, with Albert Finney playing the part in a joint production by William Gaskill and John Dexter, which afterwards became part of the National Theatre repertoire at the Old Vic.

It is a play with enormous faults, but it takes them well into its enormous stride. It has an epic sweep to it, with characters that grow to epic stature, without becoming heroic, and scenes that make a violent and vivid impact. In the Chichester production, with a beautifully simple setting by Rene Allio – representing Gilnockie's castle on one side of the stage, King James's Palace on the other, with a single tree upstage centre to stand in for the forest – it was the language and the action, as in a Shakespearean play, that evoked a rugged sense of locale without any more visual help than this from the set. No playwright since Shakespeare can have exploited a forest setting so fully, with only the density of Arden's compromise re-creation of sixteenth-century Scots to assist the illusion. But the language is as capable of suggesting the bleakness of the hills as the profusion of thickets and bracken in the forest. When Wamphray dies, pinned against the tree by the spears of the Eliots, the elder Eliot's stony farewell is:

> He will remain here on this fellside for the better nourishment of the corbies. Ride.

And again language and action combine to conjure up a vivid visual impression of the scene when Lindsay helps his mortally wounded secretary McGlass along the long road back to Edinburgh:

> LINDSAY: Ye canna mak the journey in that condition, Sandy –
> MCGLASS: I can. Observe me, sir: I'm maken it. Observe, I'm upon the road. (*He staggers round the stage, supported by Lindsay. As he goes, he sings*):

O lang was the way and dreary was the way
And they wept every mile they trod
And ever he did bear his afflictit comrade dear.
A heavy and a needless load.
A heavy and a needless load.

In the Chichester production, with a deflated Robert Stephens
supporting a staggering Frank Wiley, it seemed miles from one side
of the stage to the other. The problem of contriving a language to
write in is inseparable from the problem of writing about a primitive
society. William Gaskill put this point well in an interview he had
with Tom Milne:

> If you want to write a play about the Congo, or about Vietnam,
> and you want to include scenes of the natives speaking, what do
> you do on the English stage? Because there is no modern equiva-
> lent; you can't have them speaking their original language, you
> can't have them speaking stage West Indian, but they've got to
> speak something which makes you think they belong to a primi-
> tive community. Now, if you set it in the past, and you use a very
> rich archaic language, then you're getting there.

I don't think Arden in his writing or Gaskill and Dexter in their
production solved the problem completely. At the beginning of the
run at Chichester, a lot of the lines were incomprehensible, though
by the time the play came to the Old Vic, more concessions had been
made to the difficulties that audiences were having. Arden says that
his model was Arthur Miller's reconstruction of early American speech
in *The Crucible*. But *The Crucible* often achieved an almost poetic
concentration and expressiveness, without ever being hard for an
audience to follow. An ideal audience for *Armstrong's Last Goodnight*
would have to see the play more than once or at least read it before
going to the theatre. But while there are passages that sink far below
the lowest level of Miller's writing, there are also passages of poetry
that rise far above his highest. The love speech that the Lady makes
to Gilnockie combines simple salty images with metaphysical conceits.
As pastiche of sixteenth-century verse, this is excellent, but it's also
much more than pastiche:

E   **57**

John Arden

> When I stand in the full direction of your force
> Ye need nae wife nor carl to stand
> Alsweel beside ye and interpret.
> There is in me ane knowledge, potent, secret,
> That I can set to rin ane sure concourse
> Of bodily and ghaistly strength betwixt the blood
> Of me and of the starkest man alive. My speed
> Hangs twin with yours: and starts ane double flood:
> Will you with me initiate the deed
> And saturatit consequence thereof – ?
> Crack aff with your great club
> The barrel-hoops of love
> And let it pour
> Like the enchantit quern that boils red-herring broo
> Until it gars upswim the goodman's table and his door
> While all his house and yard and street
> Swill reeken, greasy, het, oer-drownit sax-foot fou –

And if no one who hasn't been primed is likely to know that 'quern' means hand-mill, it doesn't matter all that much.

Although the characters are still divided into groups – the Armstrongs, Lindsay and McGlass, the Lady and the Maid, the Eliots, the Clerks, the Secretaries and so on – the complex plot resolves itself more clearly than ever before into a conflict between the principal characters, Gilnockie and Lindsay. Gilnockie is the familiar Arden incarnation of anarchic libido, but in a much finer form than we have so far met it. For the first time (except in *Ironhand*) the figure is literally a robber baron. In the first scene he appears in – a very Brechtian scene, with a single self-contained incident in it – we see the treacherous side of his nature, vowing friendship with Wamphray, then disarming him while he is asleep in the forest, to leave him to be slaughtered by the father of the girl he is reputed to have raped. Then immediately we are shown the lovable side of Gilnockie. Measuring his sword against Lindsay's, or singing his defiance in a manner reminiscent of Sailor Sawney –

> I slew the King's Lieutenant
> And garr'd his troopers flee
> My name is Johnny the Armstrang
> And wha daur meddle wi' me?

he is like a naughty child with an adult power to kill. But when Lindsay refuses to be cowed, he responds with generous-spirited friendship and hospitality –

> GILNOCKIE: Break it with ye. Bread: salt. Ye are the King's Herald: ye bring the offer of the King. Acceptit! I am his Officer. Ye are ane good man. Gilnockie's roof-tree renders welcome. Welcome, sir.
> (*He shakes Lindsay's hand with ceremony.*)
> Mr Hieland Pen-and-Ink, your hand. Ye are ane good man.
> (*He shakes McGlass's hand.*)

Compared with the mature and devious Lindsay, Gilnockie is uncouth and spontaneous, capable of double dealing but almost incapable of suspecting it in others. He is ingenuous in his eagerness to be the King's officer, in his haste to show his loyalty to the King by handing over the Evangelist to the authorities, in his readiness to let the man go free when Lindsay argues with him, and later in his readiness to adopt the new faith. He has ulterior motives in his conversion, which will give him a new excuse for freebooting skirmishes to expand the Kingdom of Christ, just as he has ulterior motives for making love to the Lady – what he wants is to make Lindsay jealous – but there is still an impulsiveness and a directness in everything he does. He's brave and he's willing to commit himself fully.

Before she has even let him make love to her, the Lady has neatly summed up the difference between him and Lindsay:

> You are ane lovely lion to roar and leap, and sure wad rarely gratify all submissive ladies beneath the rampancy of your posture. You are indeed heraldic, sir. Emblazonit braid in flesh and blood, whereas David Lindsay can but do it with pen and pencil upon his slender parchment.

But just as Gilnockie is far from wholly admirable, Lindsay is far from wholly contemptible. The love of peace and order is basic to his temperament, just as the love of brawling is basic to Gilnockie's, and he's sophisticated, likeable, and capable of a high moral seriousness:

> That coat is irrelevant:
> I will wear it nae further
> Till Armstrang be brocht

John Arden

Intil the King's peace and order.
I will gang towart his house
As ane man against ane man,
And through my craft and my humanity
I will save the realm frae butchery
Gif I can, good sir, but gif I can.

But he's an intellectual and a politician, which is a dangerous combination. If Gilnockie is always getting himself too involved, Lindsay tends to keep too detached, understanding the primitive power politics of sixteenth century Scotland very well but sometimes forgetting his own vulnerable position in the field that he's playing. He knows that the English Ambassador is paying Lord Maxwell to encourage the raids of the robber barons, and, as a sop to him, Lindsay persuades the King to imprison Lord Johnstone, Maxwell's enemy. But when the two lords gang up against him, Lindsay himself is in danger, particularly as he can neither persuade the King to make Gilnockie his officer, nor persuade Gilnockie to desist from his raids. And having alienated all the Scottish factions, Lindsay flirts with the idea of a free confederation of the English and Scottish borderers on the Swiss pattern. This idea appeals to him intellectually as a solution of the political problem and it leads him into risking his neck in making overtures to the English, to see whether they would support it. But like Gilnockie, though in a different way, Lindsay is an anachronism. Gilnockie is a petty king who has to be destroyed by the bigger king in the interests of unity; Lindsay is ahead of his time, trying to apply a rational diplomacy to a crude political battlefield. In the end, he stoops to playing a trick on Gilnockie which is not worthy of the standards that he has set himself. Having failed to untie the Gordian knot, Lindsay cuts through it and leads Gilnockie into an ambush. So Gilnockie dies and Lindsay survives, guaranteed a further stint of the King's grace.

Altogether, Lindsay and Gilnockie emerge very clearly and in much greater depth than most Arden characters. We never feel that they are being deprived of their free will by the exigencies of the plot. We feel that they're reacting in character to new sets of circumstances as they arise. But we don't always feel this with the other characters.

We don't feel it, for instance, in the scene where the Eliots arrive at Gilnockie's castle just in time to see him coming out of the forest with the Lady. On the level of plot mechanics, this scene is very good. Gilnockie's wife is the elder Eliot's sister and Eliot now knows that Gilnockie has betrayed her. But the Eliots have come to persuade Gilnockie to ride with them in a raid on Salkeld. It is difficult for Gilnockie to decide, because he doesn't yet know whether the King will honour the promise that Lindsay has made on his behalf. But he feels friendship towards Lindsay and doesn't want to break faith with him. So far as Gilknockie is concerned, the cards are dramatically and effectively stacked. But with Eliot, Arden shows no interest in his personal reaction to the situation. He's a man who has killed Wamphray for sleeping with his daughter and now here he is, renewing his comradeship-in-arms with the man who has just betrayed his sister. But Arden misses his chance of bringing out the irony of the situation. He's only concerned with the plot, which requires the two men to ride together on the raid, breaking the peace that Lindsay is working for – therefore Eliot can't be allowed to quarrel with Gilnockie. At first, he doesn't even refer to the infidelity, and then, towards the end of the scene, he uses it as an extra means of putting pressure on Gilnockie:

> It is but for ancient friendship alane I hae sparit your life this day. And ye haver with me now upon resumption of that friendship? Ye hae but the ae choice, Johnny: ride wi' the Eliots, or die like a Johnstone.

The other point in the play where the action seems to have far too little to do with the free will of the characters is in the stabbing of McGlass. This is remarkably similar to the stabbing of Sparky in *Serjeant Musgrave's Dance* in that that it's obviously done deliberately but no motive for it ever comes into focus. Why should the Evangelist suddenly snatch the knife out of McGlass's belt and kill him? The only provocation is that McGlass has been pointing out the inconsistency of taking both Gilnockie, who caused Wamphray's death, and Meg, Wamphray's woman, into the same fold of penitents.

The character of the Evangelist is very unsatisfactory anyway.

John Arden

He's introduced for the sake of a rather sketchy parallel between the robber barons' resistance to the King and the Lutheran rebellion.

> Here, in this forest, they tell me, there are gentlemen that are dividit against their Princes, and brook nocht their commandments. The Prelates of the Kirk are in like manner this day with the Princes of the State. They are forgotten by God because God is forgotten of them. They are outwith His benevolence, for they wadna feed their sheep when their sheep were an-hungerit. John Armstrang – ye are ane mickle hornit ram – are ye weel-fed by your shepherds – spiritual, temporal? I trow nocht. I trow nocht.

Ian McKellen's performance in the part at Chichester showed how hopelessly at sea this good actor was in trying to make sense of the character. He's there purely as a representative of ideas. His relationship with Meg is treated very superficially and his exchanges with the cynical Lady, who is suspicious of his motives, don't add any depth to it because he doesn't have any motives. He kills McGlass because it is necessary for the play that he should. It carries the plot forward and it endorses the secretary's criticism of his master:

> Ye did tak pride in your recognition of the fallibility of man. Recognize your ain, then, Lindsay: ye have ane certain weakness, ye can never accept the gravity of ane other man's violence.

When the dying man urges Lindsay to let the King see the knife in his side, so that he will take action against Gilnockie, Lindsay doesn't demur. His attempt to counter violence without using violence has failed, just like Musgrave's. Gilknockie wasn't responsible for the Evangelist's action, but there is a curious kind of justice in the end. The trick that Lindsay plays on Gilnockie is very much like the trick that Gilnockie played on Wamphray, winning the man's trust by promises of friendship, disarming him and then letting him die. Gilnockie didn't kill Wamphray himself: Lindsay doesn't kill Gilnockie himself. But both are authors of the deaths. There is even a visual tie-up between the two scenes. In the Wamphray scene, Gilnockie and his men lie down on the ground with Wamphray and appear to fall asleep. But as soon as Wamphray is heard snoring, one by one they sit cautiously up. We know that treachery is afoot and we know

Wamphray will be the victim, but we don't yet know how. Theatrically this is very effective and the effect is echoed when the King wanders downstage, chatting to Gilnockie and offering him a drink out of his flask, while one by one Gilnockie's men are gagged and dragged silently off-stage by bare-footed Highland soldiers, leaving Gilnockie alone, unarmed and without even his piper to accompany his dying song:

> To seek het water beneath cauld ice
> Surely it is ane great follie
> I hae socht grace at a graceless face
> And there is nane for my men and me.

LEFT-HANDED LIBERTY

Left-Handed Liberty, Arden's most recent full-length play to be performed, was commissioned by the Corporation of the City of London to commemorate the 750th anniversary of the sealing of the Magna Carta. It was staged at the Mermaid Theatre in June 1965, with Patrick Wymark as King John, in a stylish production by David William.

As a play it never gets off the ground because Arden never gives the story a chance to grow. Instead of developing any one subject, or any one style, he darts about making different experiments with different styles of dramatization, but there is very little incident and very little action. He lets the characters argue with each other too much, and they have to carry the play forward by telling each other what has happened. The only one to emerge with much force is John himself, and he does this more through the direct relationship he establishes with the audience than through relationships with other characters.

The play starts promisingly enough with a prologue in which Pandulph, the papal legate, addresses the audience with the house-lights still up. Illustrating what he says with references to an astronomical chart, he announces that progress in the affairs of this world has ceased to be possible. God has withdrawn from human history, and, until the Second Coming, no improvement is to be expected, except through the Church, which will only concern itself with spiritual, not material conditions.

Pandulph talks in a pithy but dignified English which sometimes has a biblical ring to it, but the formal cadences do more to point the solemnity of the man than to suggest the period. As John Arden reminds us in his notes, he would actually have spoken in Latin, and most of the other characters would have talked to each other in Norman French. In his first scene with John, Padulph's speech seems archaic by the side of the King's, which is humorously but joltingly modern.

PANDULPH *(producing a jewelled cross)*: Wear this upon your breast in token of your sanctified intention.

JOHN: Diamonds? Good. Silver-gilt. Not so good. Parsimonious, rather.

PANDULPH: Make sure you keep your word. The Pope is a man of honour, he expects his vassals to be likewise.

JOHN: He has evidently little experience of the sort of vassal that I am lumbered with.

But a great deal of John's humour depends on the staccato phrases Arden gives him. He is always puncturing the dignity of other characters with an irony which, partly because of the cadence of the phrases, has a very modern ring. We notice this first in the scene with his mother, Queen Eleanor, who, like Pandulph, expresses herself formally, archaically, in periods very reminiscent of King James's Bible.

Now that he has inherited to the full the portions of all those other sons who came into the world before him, and who left it before him in their time and in the time of God, he should be no longer landless. Yet we have heard there are some who still describe him so. They name him Bluntsword also, King Soft-blade, is it not?

JOHN: Or even King Slapstick – that is one way I have heard it put. Very funny. Malicious. But I would not call it true. The military circumstances are –

This is from the first scene of the play, which falls immediately into the pitfall of letting the characters establish the historical background by telling each other about recent events which they would already know about. After two minutes of this, the subject of the Queen's imminent death is introduced, and the writing switches to simplified blank verse in the manner of *The Happy Haven*. But though the words are simple the meaning is often rather cryptic –

John. John. On your left hand
Wear your most beautiful ring
And do not let it show.
The military circumstances
Enforce you to be slow
But you must never be late.

John Arden

Again, as so often, we have different characters standing for different factions, different interests. Only John stands for himself. Pandulph represents the interests of the Pope, who is intent on remaining the overlord of the English King, and the Lord Mayor those of the City. We meet several of the Barons but in practice they are represented by two ringleaders, Fitzwalter and de Vesci. The Archbishop has the dual role of representing both the English Church and the Magna Carta, which he drafted. He claims that he has excluded from it the more unreasonable demands of the Barons and formulated principles which would restrain them as much as the King. And Marshal, who is 'regarded as the ancient arbiter of chivalry in this Kingdom' is, in effect, the middleman between the King and the Barons.

No doubt Arden made the right decision in focusing his play not on the events leading up to the Charter, but on the immediate aftermath. With our vague memories of school history books, most of us tend to think of the Charter as an effective curb on royal autarchy, a turning point in English progress towards democracy. As a reminder that it was nothing of the sort, Arden's play is certainly useful. He shows that neither the King nor the Barons had any serious intention of honouring it and that the sealing of the document could be nothing more than a gesture when there was no agreement about how it was to be enforced. The Charter itself provides for a council of twenty-five Barons, and there was talk of a second council to control the first, but the play doesn't make it clear whether either council was in fact ever appointed. What was more to the point was that the Barons' soldiers were occupying London, while John, who fought, like Goetz, with mercenaries, had none at his disposal. The play gives a lot of space to the negotiations between the two sides: will the Barons agree to withdraw their men from London if John disbands the mercenaries that have been collected on his behalf in Flanders, and will they agree to the Archbishop's being given charge of the Tower of London pending a settlement with the King? Both sides haggle. The Archbishop is to have the Tower for a month and the Barons will withdraw their men at the end of that time if by then the nobility, the clergy, and the judiciary have taken oaths to accept the Charter and obey the council. And the scenes of negotiation are interlarded with gobbets of history regurgitated through the mouths of John himself, Marshal, Pandulph and the Clerk.

In all this – the whole of Act One and the first scene of Act Two – there is very little action. There is one episode which is theatrically effective, when the assembled Barons refuse to stand up on the entrance of their King, and John gets them to their feet by provoking them. He then gets them to sit by sitting himself. But most of the writing is very flat, as in the scene where Fitzwalter and de Vesci are throwing dice to give a perfunctory appearance of stage action during their long argument about whether to believe John's promise that he has cancelled the order for the mercenaries. After this, Arden seems to realize that the play needs some form of relief and he treats us to a diversion with three whores. Marshal's son, who is one of the rebel Barons, sings a song which he addresses to Lady de Vesci, establishing the fact that he is in love with her, and de Vesci himself leads the others in a noisy stamping dance, singing to a reel tune.

> Oh *what* will you gie me if I knock you in the teeth, boy,
> *What* will you gie me if I kick your *gut*?
> A *knife* in the belly and a club upon the headpiece,
> *That's* what ye're wanting, it's what you'll *get*!

The arrival of the Lord Mayor pitches the action away from private relationships back into politics. He complains about the behaviour of the soldiery and the adverse effect they are having on the economy of the City. So once again the dialogue relapses into the argument of negotiation.

> MAYOR: It is not only the matter of the turbulent soldiery for which in regard to my recent outburst of anger I crave pardon – but a serious and deep consideration for our essential purposes at this time. The King has promised to govern his realm with what amounts to justice and restraint. He has taken note–
> FITZWALTER: He has been forced to take note.
> MAYOR: – of the demands of the nobility, and the church, and also the commercial interests for the first time in history. Forced, yes, my Lord, and forced by your soldiers – that is, the nobility alone. The church, when she was alone in the time of

the Interdict, failed to coerce him: and we, as men of com-
merce, are of course men of peace – we have but our wharves
and counting-houses and our profit and loss. Therefore we depend on your honour. We have let you into London for your
manifest advantage: *our* manifest advantage, my Lord, is a
complete and equitable enforcement of the entire Charter, no
clause of it bated, and with no distortion of its purposes. Are
you prepared to grant us that?

It is not until Act Two, Scene Four that we get another incident.
With John and his travelling party picnicking in a Kentish orchard
and interrupting the picnic to hear a law-suit, this scene is very
much like something out of *The Caucasian Chalk Circle*, and John's
idea of justice is rather like Azdak's. A goldsmith complains that his
wife has been living with the parish priest for five years, making him
a laughing stock in Dover, to the detriment of his business. John
fines the priest fifty shillings and orders him to pay a further fifty
shillings to the goldsmith as compensation for abducting his wife.
But the goldsmith has to pay the fifty shillings over to John as a fee
for hearing the case, and as a penalty for interrupting the picnic.
However, he is appointed a Craftsman to the Royal Household, while
the priest is allowed to keep the woman, but warned not to let the
Archdeacon hear about it. It is a pleasant, self-contained little scene,
quite irrelevant to the main action and it is something of a measure
of the play's failure that this episode sticks so much more clearly in
the memory than most of the rest.

It comes very close to the rather patchy end of Act Two. It is
followed by the arrival of young Marshal with his sword drawn.
He has discovered that John has broken faith over the mercenaries,
who are due to sail from Flanders as soon as the wind is favourable.
Pandulph then interrupts the scene by announcing to the audience
that the Pope has declared the Charter null and void, whereupon
John pulls down the copy of the Charter, which has been hanging
opposite Pandulph's chair all through the act, and the curtain falls
with young Marshal's threat that if the French King lays claim to
the English throne the Barons will support him.

In Act Three, there is even less dramatization and even more
summary than we have had so far. The act begins with some blank

verse from the Archbishop about the Tower of Babel, followed by a long argument between him and Pandulph. Pandulph threatens to suspend him unless he submits to the Pope. The Archbishop, who feels absolutely committed to the Charter, says he will go to Rome to explain it to the Pope personally, but we never hear what became of this mission. Pandulph's role as chorus-narrator is enlarged in this act. The scenes are more disparate and therefore need more linking together. Now he transports us to the French Court where we see the King, the Dauphin, and Blanche, the Dauphin's wife, planning their invasion. But the account of the war which follows is terribly sketchy, compared with the solidly established battle scenes in *Ironhand*. There is a scene with John, Marshal and Officers in which we learn from their conversation that John has been having difficulties in paying his soldiers, and that

> SECOND OFFICER: Louis controls Kent, Surrey and Sussex. The army of God –
> MARSHAL: The excommunicate Army of God –
> SECOND OFFICER: – is besieging Windsor and Dover. As before, their principal camp is London. The Scots are besieging Barnard Castle here, and Durham, here. We still have freedom of manœuvre in the midlands and south-west.

But none of this is made real for us. We meet the three whores again, and one of them sings an ironic and rather Brechtian song about Liberty, which is followed by a scene between young Marshal and the Mayor, which tells us – again through conversation – about the disaffection of the Londoners and the bad behaviour of the French soldiers who have been supplied as reinforcements. Fitzwalter, who (together with de Vesci) had faded completely from the picture, reappears in an argument with Louis, who is asking for more than the English Barons are happy to give away, and young Marshal goes over to John's side. But just as the King is about to liberate Norfolk, the play stops and John talks to the audience direct.

> There comes a time in any stage-play, when the stage itself, the persons upon it, the persons in front of it, must justify their existence – and I think this is the time now: because on the 18th of October I have to die, suffering from a surfeit of

69

John Arden

cider and peaches, which is a great joke of course, for I shall be taken short in the very moment of neither victory nor defeat – my frantic history suspended under circumstances of absolute inconclusion – King John yet again too late to control his situation. A time, I say, must come, when we stand in complete bewilderment as to what we are doing here at all. I mean – what use is this –

(He takes off his sword and throws it away, out of sight.)
Or this –

(Same business with his crown.)
Or this –

(Same business with his mantle.)
– as a means of convincing you of the human importance of what we are talking about? What use am I myself – a bogeyman or ghost seven hundred and fifty years old and still mouldering – set down to prance before you in someone else's body? What in fact have you seen tonight?

A document signed, and nobody knew what for – or at least, nobody knew or could possibly know the ultimate consequences thereof. A document repudiated, and nobody knew what for. A villainous King and his villainous Barons sprinkling each other's blood all over the map. A good Archbishop disgraced. A sagacious Pope flung all cack-handed in the Vatican by contradictory letters continually coming in on every post, from an island which he might be pardoned for believing had never been properly converted in the first place. And finally, a few little tit-bits of scandal not even proved to be historically true.

(He points to the Lady.)
I mean her, for instance. She was a rumour in certain circles in the thirteenth century, to her husband she was a pretext for a grievance: and that's about her lot. Or so you might believe. Because this play concerns Magna Carta, and Magna Carta only. The lady is peripheral. A thoroughly masculine piece of work was Magna Carta – a collaborative effort between brutal military aristocrats and virgin clergy: as you will appreciate, when I read you a certain clause from it.

And he goes on to read not only from the Charter, but from a modern history book about it by Dr William Sharp McKechnie. The lecture method has taken over completely, but John's lecture does not even remain on the historical subject. He sidetracks off on to the matter of sexual attraction, using Lady de Vesci as a kind of blackboard illustration.

> I wonder how she does walk? – two legs are common property, but to support a whole body, successfully, without conscious art and effort – did you ever see such a thing as a two-legged stool? And then she has her buttocks, above the legs, to sit on – but also to give pleasure to the eyes and to the touch. She has a womb which has brought forth more than one living child. She has her breasts which have afforded abundant nourishment to those children. She has her bowels and her heart and her lungs, her hands, her arms, her shoulders, her neck. And on her neck – look how it balances! – so small and delicate an egg of bone that I can almost encompass it within my ten fingers, and yet it is quite heavy and contains much that should give us pause. For by means of this egg alone can this creature eat, drink, talk, breathe, smell, see, weep, laugh, hear, and above all, think!

This generalized and discursive speech is not without its humour, but John has lost a lot of the brisk irony he had in the beginning. The whole play resolves itself into a debate, with Pandulph joining in, about the nature of authority and of John's resistance to the Pope's authority, which ministers to the unity of all men, as desired by Christ, and finally the discussion goes back to the original subject, the relationship between the authority of the Crown and the authority of Common Law.

The play ends with yet another change of style. The story of John's death is told partly in verse, partly in prose summary and partly in mime, extras moving about the stage with flags, drums, kit-bags and weapons. We see them dragging wagons across the mud-flats of the Wash and getting stuck.

> (*In the middle of the stage they are all staggering as though surrounded by swirling water. If possible an effect of shifting eddies should be projected on the map of the Wash behind.*)

And the last word goes to Marshal:

> The waters have come over him as the Red Sea came over Pharoah ... My son, our new King Henry is not ten years old. He has

succeeded to a kingdom all but swept away by deluge. I am too
near my own grave to be able myself to dredge it up again for
him. But one thing must be seen to. At his coronation, whatever
the Church may say, he must take oath to observe the Great
Charter. There is no other way by which the war can be stopped,
the French driven out and the King's people held together. Let
it but be done, my son, and the commonwealth may continue...

Help Landless John back
Onto his own dry land.
Never mind the wagons...
Unclench his cold left hand.

FRIDAY'S HIDING

Friday's Hiding must be the only play ever written with its stage directions in blank verse. It was finished in 1965, commissioned by the Glasgow Citizens' Theatre and performed there in March 1966.

The original suggestion was that Arden (and his wife, who collaborated) should write a play without words. In fact it has some dialogue in it, but only a minimum. It is a story about an 'auld dour skinflint of a farmer' who lives with his sister, Aunt Letty. His two labourers, Eddie and Willie Tam have worked for him for seventeen years without getting a rise, and only getting their money with great difficulty. Each pay-day, after collecting the money from the bank, he hides.

The style that the Ardens envisage is suggested by their introductory notes.

> Farmers who have a reputation for meanness are not necessarily *essentially* uncharitable people: but their resources – even today – seem so much at the mercy of unexpected accidents of nature and inexplicable falls in prices and so forth that the foolishness of letting money go which could have been kept becomes ingrained into their character. Thus it would be a serious error for the actors playing Mr and Miss Balfour to portray the one as a miserable old skinflint and the other as a dried-up sour spinster. They should much rather be the rosy-cheeked bright-eyed toy-town figures out of a child's picture book of the countryside, and let the opposite elements in their personalities arise through the action.

The expository speeches at the beginning of the play set the scene, with Aunt Letty waiting in the kitchen for her housekeeping money, and the two labourers waiting in the yard to waylay John Balfour on his way back from the bank.

Seeing that they are watching out for him, he makes his entrance concealed in a haycock. The short lines of the stage directions imitate the movements of the characters' minds.

F   73

John Arden

> The haycock sneezes.
> They turn at the noise.
> There is nocht but a haycock.
> Whaur the hell did that come from?
> They look at it – dubious –

John Balfour gets safely to the kitchen, locks away some of the money into a cash-box and puts some into his wallet. He sits down and drinks a cup of tea while the labourers, who are sitting in the yard outside, drink tea that the old woman gives them. They talk again. Eddie decides to ask for a rise. Silence ensues again as John Balfour comes to the door.

> They look wages at him, grind their teeth in wages,
> shuffle their feet (to which they are risen)
> But he takes no damn notice.
> Only indicates the dungforks
> they are to work with this afternoon and away he goes from them.
> Minding his own business, minding it severely.

They mime their work in the fields, and he mimes his, hoeing. Eddie does a comic mime of the revenge he would like to take on John Balfour, but, observed by him, has to turn a dance of triumph into the pursuit of an imaginary wasp. The action develops into a comic chase, with the labourers, hoe in hand, hot on the heels of the old man who hides behind bushes and in a ditch. When he finally falls over and they jump in on him, they think they have killed him, and contritely take his motionless body back to the farmhouse. They lay him out, with a cloth on his face, and Aunt Letty, having relieved the old man of his keys, makes the two labourers a cup of tea. Reviving, John Balfour finally puts the two men's wages on the mantelpiece. Summoning all his courage, Eddie demands a rise, which produces rage and consternation. Angrily Aunt Letty throws all three men out of the kitchen, and left alone, she dresses up in her mother's old wedding-dress which she has kept in a chest. Spying on her through the window, John Balfour decides to marry her off to Willie Tam. The three of them get in again. John Balfour recovers his keys and slyly puts the money back from the mantelpiece into the cash-box. The play ends with a song, of which the final chorus becomes a round song.

> THEN LET US DRINK AND NEVER THINK
> WE CAN OURSELVES IMPROVE OUR LIFE
> UNLESS THE MASTER TAKE THE LEAD
> WE SHALL FIND NOCHT BUT GRIEF AND STRIFE.
> CHORUS:
> WE SHALL FIND NOCHT WE SHALL FIND NOCHT
> TILL EVERY MAN CONTROLS HIS WIFE
> TILL EVERY FORK LIES UNDER THE KNIFE
> TILL EVERY PLATE KENS ITS PLACE IN THE LARDER
> AND EVERY SLATE STICKS TO THE RAFTER
> AND ONE GANGS FIRST AND THE REST GANG AFTER
> THAT'S WHAT WE CALL RESTORING ORDER.

But as they sing, Aunt Letty takes off the wedding-dress and puts it back in the chest. As the farmer's sister, we are meant to infer, she would never really have married a hired labourer.

After the wordiness of so much of *Left-Handed Liberty* it is interesting to see Arden experimenting with the idea of using a minimum of words. *Friday's Hiding* doesn't add up to very much in itself, but maybe he will go on to write a full-length play which will capitalize on the experiments he made in it, and in *Ars Longa, Vita Brevis*.

THE ROYAL PARDON

The Royal Pardon ranks with Robert Bolt's *The Thwarting of Baron Bolligrew* as one of the best plays for children in existence. But there is much in it that only the most sophisticated children could fully understand. 'In our experience,' the Ardens write in their preface, 'children prefer to be occasionally puzzled by the behaviour of adults in plays, as this bears out their observations of life outside the theatre.'

The plot is complex, with many sequences that emerge tangentially out of what went before, as is often the way with plays that originate partly out of improvization. But the whole play is full of physical action, often violent, often funny, so there is plenty for even the youngest children to enjoy, without necessarily understanding quite what all the rumpus is about.

Many of Arden's familiar preoccupations underpin the play's unusual structure and it is typical that the two main protagonists should be a policeman and a soldier. The Constable – the role Arden played himself at the amateur première – is an absurd figure of killjoy authoritarianism. Although the play belongs to no specific historical period, he represents a mixture of Puritanism and Victorianism. The soldier is not quite a pacifist or an anarchist but he is vociferous about opinions which carry him a long way in both directions. He rather resembles the soldier in Whiting's *A Penny for a Song*, who comes home from the French wars wanting to tell the King of England that they ought to be stopped, but Luke, Arden's soldier, actually talks to the King.

> Starving though we were and tired and ill
> We never did forget our soldier's skill:
> We kept our boots clean and our bayonets bright,
> We waved our banners and we marched upright,
> We dared the French to meet us and to fight.
> And when we met we fought till none could stand.
> Our bodies now lie in a foreign land,
> Defeated, they have said. But we know better:

We obeyed our general's orders to the letter.
If blame there is to be – indeed we did not win –
Blame not your loyal soldiers, gracious King,
But blame those ministers, who sitting warm at home
Sent us across the seas, unfed, unclothed, alone,
To do our duty the best way that we could.
We did it, sir, by pouring out our blood.
There is no more to say.

Most of the play is in prose but there are passages like this – which are intended to stand out – in rhyme, and there are several songs, some in rhyming verse and some in blank verse. There is also a great deal of doggerel in the scenes we see being rehearsed by Mr and Mrs Croke and their troupe of strolling players.

MRS CROKE: Nay, should he find us here, his angry blade
  Must pierce thy heart and thou on turf be laid.
  Sweet knight, there is such peril in thy devotion
  I sorely fear it will destroy this nation.
CROKE: Yet am I not still loyal to the crown?
  I swear it, by this rose that I pluck down!

The Constable's first function in the play is to interrupt a performance by the troupe and to arrest William, one of the actors, who is cheeky to him. He whistles for his comic Under-Constable, who comes on in his underpants, followed by his comic wife, who is trying to mend a hole in his trousers. A good deal of comic dialogue and comic business follows, rather in the style of a music-hall sketch. Luke is beaten up by the two policemen and thrown into gaol together with William. Mr and Mrs Croke – through whom Arden satirizes the selfishness of the old-style actor-managers – do nothing to help but William is reprieved by a Royal Pardon which is extended to all actors, together with a summons to appear before the King. And Luke escapes thanks to Esmeralda, the company's juvenile lead and general utility girl.

The next phase of the plot is concerned with Luke's efforts to get himself accepted as a member of the company. Not because of Esmeralda, who seems far more partial to him than he to her, but because he thinks the masks and costumes that the actors wear will

John Arden

help him to evade the Constable, who is in pursuit of him. The Crokes, even though they need an extra man, are very snooty about taking on a non-professional – until Luke demonstrates how much the artist depends on the artisan. Their scenery keeps falling down and he repairs it.

The rehearsal sequence in which this point is made is rather long for children. Parts of it can be made extremely funny in performance but much of the satire on the airs and affectations of the actor-manager will inevitably be above their heads.

> No, no, it's altogether too difficult to do it without props. I must have the rose – I have to smell it and kiss it, and put it in your bosom and so forth – trellis, Esmeralda, trellis, if you please. The imagery of the rose is of prime importance to this scene – William, are you watching? You may find yourself playing Lancelot one of these days: learn, me boy, learn – there's a tradition in this part, you know, as in all the great classic parts – we ignore it at our peril.

But we return to the excitement of the chase when the Constable appears and Luke evades him by putting on a mask. All through the rest of the play this pursuit theme provides suspense. Even when the King sends the troupe to Paris to perform at the French court, the Constable is able to persuade him to let him go across the channel in pursuit of the dangerous 'murderer'. He has convinced himself that Luke, who hit him over the head with a bottle during a chase, was at least 'attempting' murder.

Beside the romantic interest of the Luke–Esmeralda relationship, there is another romance between the English Prince and the French Princess. Both Kings warn their children that it is only a marriage of political convenience. They must not fall in love with each other in case it is expedient to dissolve it in a few years' time. But as soon as the French King leaves him alone with the Princess, the young Prince shows himself capable of passion:

> Yours and no-one else's is the fruit that I must pluck.
> Therefore, as I cram its fragrant pulp between my teeth
> Let me not pause for a moment's heedful breath –

Let me tell myself rather 'Between this instant and my death
There can be no pleasure equal to what I now feel.
Let me not scatter peel nor pip nor core
Upon the ground to remind me that I could have eaten yet
more.'
I shall swallow you whole
If only for a while:
Let us both tell our children
That we ate and we were full.

It is interesting though that the Ardens find it necessary to make him
look more like a prole than a prince.*

Your hands are thick and red
They would cut meat as well as bread
You have upon your shoulders a strong round head
Would thrust itself into a wall and break the bricks and mortar
down:
Your body is the body of a hod-carrying clown
And yet you speak in sweet words like the son of a true king.

Their romance has only a small part, though, in the second half of
the play which is chiefly concerned with a plot of the French actors to
poison the English, so that they will themselves win the prize the
French King is offering for the winning performance. The poison
severely indisposes the Crokes, who eat greedily of the French food,
and it has its effect on Esmeralda, who eats some of it, just to spite
Mrs Croke who tries to appropriate her share when the girl says she
isn't hungry. Only Luke, who in true working-class fashion has
brought sandwiches, is immune to the effects of the poison. It is
therefore he who has to carry the performance, which he does in a
heroically sustained improvization

The Constable meanwhile has got himself into bad odour with the
Prince and Princess by mistaking her for Luke in disguise and the

* Of course this may have been written because of the actor who played the
part at Beaford. Similarly, the Clown who appears as a member of the troupe in
Act One is written out of Act Two because at Beaford the actor was needed to
play an officer at the French court.

John Arden

Prince for an actor with a cardboard crown on his head.* This theme of confusion between reality and stage fiction is developed in the scene of Luke's improvization. The Constable who has been beaten up and thrown downstairs by the irate Prince is deranged by the blows to his head and he arrives on stage with a real sword to chase Luke who has to fight him off with a theatrical sword. As a character in his improvized play, Luke is wearing a crown and when he runs out of the hall, the Constable, in his confused state, advances with his sword on the Princess, who is also wearing a Crown. Luke, returning, makes her, the King and the Prince all take their crowns off and his verse speech (in which he hypnotizes the Constable with a pair of scissors) reminds us that the play we are watching is no less unreal than the play-within-the-play. It also reminds us that *The Royal Pardon* had its origin in bedtime stories that the Ardens told their children.

> Cardboard and paper and patches and glue
> Pleated and crumpled and folded in two
> With a pair of white fingers and a little bit of skill
> We make a whole world for the children to kill.
> Prop them up on the table and set them in a row
> And from the far corner lean your face out and blow
> They'll all tumble down, both the sword and the crown
> And the glittering gold weathercocks on the towers of the town.
> After they've fallen the clouds will grow dark
> And the children will creep home from the cold empty park
> The raindrops will soak the wet cardboard into mud
> Will soak the hard crust on your butterless bread
> And the clothes on your back and the shoes where you tread –
> Then the sheets on the bed
> Then the leaves on the trees
> Wetter than the warm wet westerly breeze –
> So lie down, lie, lie and grow dry
> Wrapped in a blanket and drowsy your eye.
> Tomorrow you'll cry and tomorrow you can weep
> All you need now is to fall fast asleep. . . .

* At Beaford the actor actually wore a cardboard crown but when it dropped on the floor a metallic clang was produced by the musicians who accompanied the whole action with sound effects and some of the speeches with a tapped out rhythm.

THE TRUE HISTORY OF SQUIRE
JONATHAN AND HIS
UNFORTUNATE TREASURE

The True History of Squire Jonathan and His Unfortunate Treasure,
a very short piece performed at a lunch-hour theatre club in June
1968, was not written for children but it belongs to the same vein as
The Royal Pardon and it is also set in a period which is legendary
rather than historical. According to the stage directions, 'the style of
the decor and costumes is what one might call "Grimm-fairy-tale-
Gothic"'. They also prescribe that the Squire is dressed in 'clothes
which have once been quite splendid but are now soiled, threadbare
and patched'. Ed Berman, who directed the play, stressed the political allusions by dressing the Blonde Woman, who later strips, as
Britannia.

Some of the dialogue is in verse but the best speech – which is one
of the best-written in all Arden's work – is in prose. It comes at the
beginning when Jonathan talks directly to the audience.

> I am a small man and nothing about me is large. Look at me. My
> features are small, confined and tight. My hair is red – an un-
> becoming red – I do not want to hear anybody say it is the
> colour of the hair of Judas. My teeth are good, hard, yellow, not
> large, but sharp – as sharp and as dangerous as those of an
> unreliable dog. When provoked I can bring them together very
> suddenly indeed and very cruelly. I have in my time taken bites
> out of the backs of ankles. Malignant ankles. And I am prepared
> to do so again if my personal convenience is threatened. If I
> were to remove my clothes – if I were to remove them (which I
> do not intend to do) – yet – if I were – I say – to remove my
> clothes, you would be confronted with a body as cadaverous as
> it is hairy, with ribs like prongs of a garden fork, a navel like an
> egg-cup full of dust, a ridiculously wrinkled pair of cullions, and
> a well-loved drooping yard that very badly desires employment.
> Employment other than that afforded it periodically by my own
> unsatisfied fingers. I also have flat feet. The total aspect of my

John Arden

person would in fact be absurd and unlikely to give pleasure to any woman save for the most depraved: unless she were able, by the intensity of her spirit, to peer right through the flesh of this rotten carcase and to discern within it the intensity of *my* spirit, my small spirit, a bluebottle fly whirring and gyrating in the prison of a glass jar.

He opens the box which contains his treasure but it is worthless to him, he tells us, without his 'mountain of a white woman' for whom he has been waiting fifteen years. During these years he has seen no one but the sinister Dark Men, who wear tattered hats and walk with long sticks and threaten him from outside his window.

At last he sees a big woman riding by on a horse. By startling the horse with a rude noise, he makes her fall off. At first he refuses to let her in but after he has shut his treasure box and pushed it out of the way, he opens the door and unctuously offers help. Soon he has opened the box again and he gives her jewels from it as he encourages her to take her clothes off until she is wearing nothing but a large chastity belt, of which she says the key is lost. She tries to encourage him to break it open but he not only refuses, he becomes more and more abusive, convinced that she has come only to make a laughing stock of him and that she will go off with the Dark Men when they call for her. She gives him back his jewels, using a brooch to pick open the lock on the chastity belt, which comes off. Jonathan threatens her with a knife but she warns him that if he kills her, her corpse will be too heavy for him to lift.

She jumps out of the window and they catch her on a blanket, cheering and laughing and shouting their thanks to Jonathan in the same diluted Scots dialect Arden used in *Armstrong's Last Goodnight*. The play ends rather inconclusively as Jonathan notices that one piece of jewellery she hasn't returned is the gold belt he put around her middle:

> It made creases in her flesh.
> It was scarcely to her advantage.
> She might as well keep it.
> I am not yet defeated.

THE HERO RISES UP

Several years before *The Hero Rises Up* was produced at the Round House, John Arden accepted a commission to write a musical about Nelson for the West End. I have no means of judging how far the script used at the Round House differs from what he originally wrote but I must try to judge the script separately from the production, which was very bad. It was done by John Arden and Margaretta D'Arcy themselves, with Bettina Jonic as Lady Hamilton, Henry Woolf as Nelson and a weak supporting cast. It was accompanied by a non-stop light show given by the Sensual Arts Laboratory. This made it very hard to concentrate on the words which in any case were hard to hear, thanks partly to the difficult acoustics of the hall but mainly to the stylized, half-shouting delivery the authors had encouraged. The seats were unreserved and the number of tickets sold far exceeded the number of seats available so many of the audience were crouching or perching in uncomfortable positions. Bettina Jonic, a trained opera singer, projected her songs operatically while the rest of the cast sang in the way non-singing actors always do sing when they have to. Henry Woolf is only five foot tall and Miss Jonic's singing voice combined with her height to make Lady Hamilton dominate Nelson in a very strange way.

The 'Asymmetrical Authors' Preface' in the published script provides some clues towards answering the question of how far this disastrously anarchic production corresponded to the authors' intentions. They draw a distinction between two sets of tendencies which they label 'rectilinear' and 'curvilinear'. Symmetry, efficiency, the desire to impose order or 'do things properly' are *rectilinear*. When they came to Britain, the rectilinear Romans refused to allow the native (and curvilinear) Celts to go on 'muddling through'. And according to the Ardens, Nelson, who had a passionately curvilinear temperament, was committed to a rectilinear career. His energy and courage were wasted on a life of killing.

What this adds up to saying is that the Nelson the Ardens admire is not the historical Nelson, who, like everyone else, is conditioned by

John Arden

the needs and pressures of the society that he lives in, but an ideal Nelson – their idea of what he might have been if history hadn't made him into what he was. In my view, it is as pointless to try to disentangle his energy and his courage from the use he made of them in his naval career as to try to disentangle Hitler's energy and courage from his other characteristics or from his actions. The historian cannot meaningfully distinguish between what a man *is* and what he *does*. There may be a way in which the playwright can make this distinction but in *The Hero Rises Up*, the Ardens have not only failed to find it, they have failed to make any serious attempt.

> We meant to write a play which need not be *done properly*. That is to say: we wanted to produce it ourselves, so that it would present the audience with an experience akin to that of running up in a crowded wet street on Saturday night against a drunken red-nosed man with a hump on his back dancing in a puddle, his arms around a pair of bright-eyed laughing girls, his mouth full of inexplicable loud noises.

It is true that a spectacle like this makes an impact which you do not easily forget. But nor do you feel like sitting down and watching it for three hours.

The Ardens' Nelson certainly makes an initial impact when he jumps on to the stage through a paper screen, like a circus dog through a hoop, and when he starts haranguing the audience. But the dialogue they write for him is so aggressively anti-heroic and so school-masterish that the actor inevitably becomes a man talking about Nelson rather than an embodiment of Nelson.

> If you don't know who I am you ought to be ashamed of yourselves, God damn your eyes. You are, I take it, Englishmen? Is there any point in my informing you of all the great deeds I have done for you? My victories? St Vincent, the Nile, Copenhagen, Trafalgar? Of the techniques by which I achieved them? Surely all such history is already sufficiently known. I was the first naval commander who understood – and put into practice – the theory of the entire and total destruction of the enemy fleet, at whatever cost to my own. A destruction made possible by my enthusiastic disregard of everybody's orders – the orders of my immediate superiors, and also the unwritten but potent

orders provided by two hundred years of conservative naval tradition.

This is a technique which might get labelled 'Brechtian' – but only by critics who misunderstand Brecht, who made quite sure that his Galileo was acceptable to the audience as an incarnation of Galileo. He put in alienation effects which help to give a perspective on the social conditioning which is an integral part of the historical process, but he would never try to make a historical character stand outside history to give the audience a lecture. Nor would he have done anything so dramaturgically crude as to make Nelson express a point of view which is critical of Nelson's point of view.

The general level of the writing in the Ardens' play is very much lower than usual. Verse and songs are intermixed with prose dialogue in the usual way. Historical and apocryphal incidents are reproduced, partly through narrative, with one of the characters as narrator, and partly through dramatization. The selection of incidents and the allocation of space are extremely quirky. The incident of Caracciolo and the King of Naples gets twice as much space as the Battle of Trafalgar and neither get as much as the party in Act Two. This scene exploits the Nelson–Lady Nelson–Lady Hamilton triangle in a way that produces a few genuinely dramatic moments and I can envisage a production in which these moments could be made moving. What I cannot envisage is a production in which the various effects which the play could make would add together in any useful or compelling way. The curvilinear Ardens could retort that what they wanted to create was a muddle and my rectilinear answer would be that they have succeeded.

CONCLUSION

Something ought to be said in conclusion, but how can any conclusion be reached about John Arden at this stage of his career? Every play is a new departure. Although he's the most traditional of all our playwrights, in the sense of being the one who is most deeply and most profitably in touch with literary and dramatic tradition, English and foreign, he also gives himself more freedom than anyone else, both from theatrical convention and from the precedent of his own writing. The only prediction it's safe to make about his future development is that it will be fascinating to watch. Even if, some time during the next ten years, fashion suddenly swings in his direction, as it did round about 1959–60 in Pinter's, it is unlikely to affect him. Whatever happens, he is certain to go on using his plays as a means of saying what he feels he has to say, and this will never be cut and dried. His mind is too powerful, original, lively and wide-ranging. Together with his historical imagination, his social consciousness and his social conscience are more highly developed than any other English playwright's and in his plays he makes the simultaneous effort to clarify his own thinking and that of his audience. This is basically what differentiates his work from Pinter's, quite apart from all the questions of breadth and depth and complexity of poetic language and absorption with the surface of everyday behaviour. The incisiveness of Pinter's dialogue and his stage effects derives from an appearance of having thought out exactly what it is that he wants to get across, whereas Arden often seems not to know what he thinks until he sees what he writes. It is not just a matter of seeing both sides of the question. Musgraves's vacillations in the market-square scene are partly Arden's own vacillations. He uses the process of writing to attain a focus and so the focus is not there when, technically, it is needed. The only plays that are stylistically consistent and that can't be faulted structurally are two very contrasted pieces, the early *Live Like Pigs* and the short *Ars Longa, Vita Brevis*. These are both experimental plays but plays in which he does not seem to be experimenting. So far, Osborne and Pinter have not only achieved more commercial success, they have succeeded better in packaging what they have presented, but it is highly unlikely that either of them will ever write a play that can be called great. They both get out of breath too quickly. Arden lacks Osborne's immediacy of emotional appeal and Pinter's technical discipline, but if he can go on to bring off a play which combines the seriousness of *Serjeant Musgrave's Dance* and the sweep of *Armstrong's Last Goodnight* with the density and humour of *Ars Longa, Vita Brevis,* the structural control of *Live Like Pigs* and the poetry of his writing at its best, it will be a great play.

How he goes on to develop will depend largely on what or whom he writes for. There is something in his talent or in his temperament that inclines him to gravitate away from the centre of things. It is pleasing that a play as good as *The Business of Good Government* should be written for amateurs to perform in a village church and that he should spend time organizing a home-made festival at Kirbymoorside. Nor are these experiences unfruitful. According to Albert Hunt, who directed a successful production of *Ars Longa, Vita Brevis* with a group of students from an art college, one of the germs of the play was a box of old clothes that the Ardens got from a local junk yard. They put it in a shed outside their Kirbymoorside cottage for local children to come and improvise in costume. Arden obviously learns from children rather in the way that Benjamin Britten does, and the Glasgow Citizens' Theatre has almost become his Aldeburgh, but it is an enormous pity that the Royal Shakespeare Theatre has only flirted with him and that his affair with Chichester and the National Theatre hasn't developed into a marriage. What he needs more than anything is a permanent relationship with a theatre like this. If he had the chance of working on his scripts over an eight-week rehearsal period in close association with a good director, good actors, and a good 'literary manager' like Kenneth Tynan he might be able to iron out the inconsistencies and eliminate the dull patches and the structural excrescences that result from exploring ideas in a self-indulgent way. He certainly has the stuff of greatness in him; whether it ever comes out may depend more on the way the English theatre treats him than on anything within his own control.

POSTSCRIPT

This 'Conclusion' was written in 1966 – before the last three chapters. The only addition I would like to make is the pessimistic one that there now seems to be less ground for hoping that Arden will achieve a relationship with a major theatre or realize his full potential as a playwright. The plays he has written in collaboration with his wife are not so good as his earlier plays and, feeling perhaps rejected by the British Theatre, he is, in turn, rejecting it – tending more and more to operate outside it or on the fringe of it. The blurb on the backs of *The Royal Pardon* and *The Hero Rises Up* says that the Ardens 'have been consistently interested in extending the range of drama outside the conventional theatre'. This implies a continuity between the plays written for it and the plays written outside it. The danger is that so far as Arden's own work is concerned, this continuity, already attenuated, will be severed completely and that his own range as a playwright, instead of being widened, will be narrowed.